SOCIAL WORKERS AND THEIR PRACTICE IN WELFARE
BUREAUCRACIES

Social Workers and their Practice in Welfare Bureaucracies

DAVID HOWE
University of East Anglia

Gower

© David Howe 1986

All rights reserved. No part of this publication may be reproduced, stored in a retrieval system, or transmitted in any form or by any means, electronic, mechanical, photocopying, recording, or otherwise without the prior permission of Gower Publishing Company Limited.

Published by
Gower Publishing Company Limited
Gower House, Croft Road, Aldershot, Hants GU11 3HR,
England

Gower Publishing Company
Old Post Road, Brookfield, Vermont 05036,
USA

ISBN 0 566 05091 9

Printed in Great Britain

Contents

Acknowledgements — vi

1. Introduction — 1
2. The Stratification of Social Workers and their Work — 5
3. Ditching the Dirty Work — 20
4. Who is Doing What with Whom? — 35
5. Controlling the Content of Practice — 59
6. The Control and Organisation of Work — 95
7. Managerial Control — 101
8. Professional Control — 114
9. Controlling the Meaning of Welfare Work — 122
10. The Rise of the Welfare Manager — 141
11. Occupational Control and the Nature of Social Work — 158

Bibliography — 165

Acknowledgements

The help and goodwill of several hundred social workers and their managers from the six SSDs who took part in the research is greatly appreciated. Martin Davies was a regular and valued source of advice, guidance and stimulation. His continued interest encouraged me throughout the whole project. The book has been typed by Joan Mills and I am most grateful for her care, skill and patience.

1 Introduction

I seek to understand the practice of social work by examining the ways in which fieldworkers and their work are organised in Social Services Departments (SSDs).

THE SEPARATION OF PRACTICE AND ORGANISATION

Social workers experience SSDs to be organised along bureaucratic lines. This form of organisation, they feel, constrains their practice. Displays of 'true' social work by autonomous professionals are denied clear expression in the unsympathetic, even hostile environment of today's large welfare bureaucracies. Arguments of this kind do not see any necessary connection between an occupation's practice and the form of its organisation. Bureaucratic SSDs seem designed to frustrate social work's full blossoming; they are perceived as a perverse imposition.

On the other hand, it is possible to point out that social work practice is nearly always accommodated in departments which are bureaucratically organised. Why should this be? What is it about social work that encourages this type of organisation? What is the relationship between what social workers do and the structural arrangements to help them do it? All too often when discussing social work, talk about practice is kept separate from consideration of the organisation of welfare work.

Social workers in SSDs find that the shape and content of their actual practice is the result of what they like to do, what they have to do and what they can do. Professionally preferred practices may lead to family therapy or group work while statutory demands often require workers to investigate and judge people and their conduct. High referral rates leave little time for anything but the provision of a basic service. The limited number of places in a local day centre restricts the days an elderly client can be looked after away from her own home. In ways such as these it can be seen that the policies and organisation of welfare have a pervasive bearing on what takes place between worker and client when they meet.

THE SEPARATION OF OBSERVATION AND THEORY

The major empirical enquiries into the fieldwork practices of SSDs have yielded data of two types. First, quantitative information about the type, amount and direction of fieldwork activity has provided a measurable outline of social work practice. Goldberg et al. (1977 and 1978), for example, give a very useful statistical account of area team work. Second, qualitative information about the feelings and experiences of social workers offers an impressionistic picture of life in SSDs. Anecdotal evidence, such as that reported in the study directed by Stevenson and Parsloe (1978), is used to convey a 'practitioner's view'.

Essentially, both styles of reporting are written at the level of description. There is no explicit theoretical framework in which to locate the data. Hence, neither study attempts or even allows an explanation of what was seen or found. So, the question of 'what is going on in SSD area field teams?' is answered, but the question which asks 'why are things as they are?' is left largely unanswered. The need to link an explicit theory with observations made is critical to the development of any understanding which seeks to relate the characteristics of both welfare practice and the organisation of welfare work within the same conceptual schema. What social workers do and with whom they do it has to be analysed beyond the limits of professionally based practice theories. By understanding the form and style of SSDs at the level of both individual practice and broad organisational design, the book concludes that the critical characteristics of social work practice are generated within welfare bureaucracies and do not derive from the prescriptions of professional social workers.

THE INTEGRATION OF DESCRIPTION AND EXPLANATION

The way situations and events are seen, understood, approached and handled depends on how the individual is 'making sense' of them. In order to 'make sense' perceptions are categorised, ordered and related. Such impositions on our world amount to theories about how things are. Theories also act as blinkers, 'preventing the observer from being dazzled by the full-blown complexity of ... events' (Hall and Lindsey 1957, p.14). Different theories may give different accounts of the same phenomena although it may be felt by particular observers (say social workers or managers or politicians) that some theories 'account' for things better than others. It will be apparent therefore, that the research process is particularly sensitive to the pervasive nature of theory.

For most of the time our everyday world makes sense. But for the researcher there is a deliberate attempt to puzzle over the way things are, even 'obvious' and taken-for-granted matters. It may also be that old theories no longer account for what is going on, especially if new phenomena are being recognised which do not fit into our scheme of things. Or it may be that new theoretical appreciations have been acquired which disturb previous perceptions or suggest new ways of understanding what we see. For example, if social workers are understood to be professionals and professionalism is said to entail an altruistic service ethic, then differences in the skills and responses meted out to different client groups might be explained in terms of the intrinsic differences between client groups. However, if all occupational groups, including social workers, are seen to be self-seeking, promoting their own interests, then the different responses meted out to different client groups could receive an entirely different interpretation. Certainly the adoption of a new theoretical perspective may cause questions to be asked as 'old' observations and experiences are re-viewed.

I propose to consider a variety of descriptions, concepts and explanations as they are used to understand social work practice in welfare organisations. These provide a structure to the book whose argument is developed through three stages.

In the first stage, chapters 2 to 5 describe the distribution of social workers and their practices amongst the main client groups of SSDs. Field social workers are observed at three empirical levels: (1) at the broadest level, the ways in which fieldworkers are distributed and organised amongst client groups, (2) in the middle range, the types of activity carried out by different fieldworkers across client groups, and (3) at the specific level, the range and types of response displayed by fieldworkers within particular cases. These observations serve as an answer to the questions 'who is doing what with whom?' and 'why are they doing what they do?'

In the second stage, chapters 6 to 8 introduce a number of theoretical concepts on organisational form and the control of work. These help achieve a clearer understanding of two major types of occupational control: managerial control and professional control.

In the third stage, chapters 9 to 11 use the theoretical concepts to 'make sense' of the empirical observations which describe the differential distribution of social workers and their practices. The integration of data and theory provokes an unconventional view of the nature of social work. Within this view, the rise of the welfare manager is observed, trailing behind him the idea that the meaning of social work is a highly contested notion.

2 The stratification of social workers and their work

BACKGROUND TO THE RESEARCH ENQUIRY

In the mid-1970s I changed jobs. From being a social worker and team leader in a local authority Social Services Department I became a lecturer in social work. My career in social work had also spanned the large scale changes in the organisation of the personal social services that took place in 1971. As a result of the Local Authority Personal Social Services Act of 1970 I stopped being a child care officer in a children's department and on 1 March 1971 became a social worker in an SSD though I remained at my old desk in the same office with the same caseload.

These facts describe the early background to the present enquiry. It was the time of the 'Seebohm' reorganisations which witnessed field social workers coming to grips with vast increases in their range of work. It was also the time social work educators were trying to discover the right formula for the production of 'generic' practitioners, many of whom would be working in SSDs.

The two events, linked both practically and philosophically, represented a considerable expansion both in the number of social workers employed and in the potential area of practice for individual social workers. In times of expansion the stretching that takes place in an occupation's fabric reveals the underlying structure and resources upon which new developments occur. How social workers, as individuals and as an occupational group were faring in this period of very rapid growth emerged as a background question that was to trigger more specific enquiries.

The question itself was born of an interest in the way occupational groups organise and pattern their own practices. It was further stimulated by a belief that insights into the nature of a particular kind of work can be gained from understanding the ways in which those occupations carrying out the work are organised. In other words, the emergence and early evolution of LA SSDs provided a promising opportunity to study two intimately related subjects: the organisation of social workers as an occupational group and the nature of their practice.

COMING TOGETHER: THE SEARCH FOR UNITY IN THEORY AND PRACTICE

The 1960s and 1970s found social workers in an integrative frame of mind, seeking ways of coming together in thought, deed and company. There were regular attempts to fuse social work's theories and practice into a coherent whole. Unification was in the air and was recognisable on three fronts:

(1) There was professed value in offering social work as a community and family based practice which had a preventative outlook. The differences between client groups based on age and circumstance should not be the starting point for social work practice.

(2) Hopes were expressed that the two main strands in personal social service work would merge:

> The first is the mainly social democratic tradition of social work. It has its roots in Christianity, voluntary action, reform, and medical, social, and behavioural science ... A second strand is the tradition of local government welfare, with its emphasis on administrative and political control through a bureaucratic system, economic and political constraint and a knowledge base of common sense experience. (Payne 1979, p.17)

Historically these traditions provided two distinct forms of help for different clienteles. The probation service, children's departments and psychiatric social work services found themselves within the social work tradition. In contrast, work with the elderly and handicapped remained firmly in the welfare tradition. By bringing the two traditions together the intention was that those who were old, young or disabled might receive a common social work service in which needs would not be prejudged on the basis of the client's chronological, physical or mental condition.

(3) There were regular efforts to produce a unified social work theory upon which a 'unitary' practice could be based (e.g. Goldstein 1973). The prospect of a common base upon which to practise also held out the hope that social workers might gain a common identity. The more convinced social workers became about the universal core to their various practices, the more inappropriate seemed the departmental divisions between work with the young, old and handicapped. In the 1960s the professional unification of social work was gathering speed. By 1970 the British Association of Social Workers had been formed, bringing together a wide range of smaller associations including the Association of Child Care Officers, the Association of Psychiatric Social Workers and the Society of Mental Welfare Officers.

In this climate, it seemed that social workers could operate within a coherent organisational framework, practice with theoretical integrity and speak with one professional voice. The efforts to fuse social work's intellectual base and to overcome the divisiveness of handling clients by separate departments were clearly appreciated by the Seebohm Committee. Of course, it was realised that it would take a while before the full generic flavour of new practices could be achieved, but the ultimate condition of the service and its workers was thought to be in little doubt: 'The existing divisions are bound to influence the way the department works when it is first set up, but it will only work well if a serious effort is made to break down the divisions from the beginning.' (Seebohm Report 1968, p.162). Ideas, philosophies and practices were all to be welded into a common endeavour. In a sense, this marked social work's coming of age. What was still not known, however, was how the occupation would turn out as a maturing enterprise.

THE SEEBOHM REPORT AND THE ESTABLISHMENT OF SOCIAL SERVICES DEPARTMENTS

Roughly 75 per cent of all field social workers in England and Wales now work for Social Services Departments. Gathered in such numbers within these organisations, the evolution and development of the occupation becomes a subject of interest.

The interpretation made by most Social Services Departments of the Seebohm Report's message 'let us come together' was often inclined to be over enthusiastic. For many the word from Seebohm came to read 'let us come together and act as one'. This understanding particularly affected field social workers who soon found themselves dealing with almost the whole range of the department's incoming work. That such an interpretation could be made was reasonable enough. The Report, as well as spelling out its interest in a single, unified Social Services Department, also dropped broad hints that individual social workers should address themselves to a wide range of matters that previously would have been handled by not only separate workers, but separate departments. 'As a general rule, and as far as possible, a family or individual in need of social care should be served by a single worker' (p.163). Both the department and the individual social worker should adopt a comprehensive approach to the social problems of their clients in order to escape the rigid classifications implied in the symptom-centred approach of the old departments. 'Most workers in the present separate departments', the Report believed, 'could undertake a substantially wider range of work than at present' (p.163). Such a worker became known as a 'generic' social worker; one who would be working with client groups across the board.

So it was that in these early post-Seebohm days, the new local authority social worker might expect to find herself dealing with a mentally handicapped adult, a request to have a six year old child received into care, the accommodation difficulties of a recently discharged psychiatric patient, and the problems besetting a severely arthritic eighty year old lady, all during the course of a working day, albeit a busy one.

FIRST DOUBTS

An early study by the DHSS (1975, p.10) noted that in SSDs there had been a 'first flush of "everyone doing everything"'. Given some of the injunctions of the Seebohm Report (such as 'the kind of worker we expect to emerge will be one who has had a generic training ... to cope with a whole range of social need' p.163), this seemed a not unreasonable interpretation. But doubts about the continued ability or likelihood of social workers maintaining such occupational homogeneity led to two research questions, colloquially phrased but reflecting the scepticism emerging over the likely prevalence of 'generic' practice:

> 'Surely everyone isn't doing everything?' asked of field social workers in the area teams of SSDs.

> 'And if everyone isn't doing everything', the query persists, 'then who is working with whom?'

These questions were posed in the late 1970s. By then other people were becoming interested in the way things were working out in SSDs. Still not much was known about these new and large organisations, so little in fact that a contributor to the Social Policy Year Book in 1977 could write 'It is not known how workloads are distributed between workers of different skills' (McCreadie 1977, p.46). The distribution of social workers remained 'uncharted research territory'. But there were people beginning to map the new terrain and who were 'frankly sceptical' (Stevenson and Parsloe 1978, p.199) about the feasibility of undifferentiated practice so widely assumed to be present in the organisation of SSD fieldwork.

SETTLING DOWN AND SETTLING OUT

Researchers were faced with a rich opportunity to examine, for the first time, local authority fieldworkers operating as an integrated group in large numbers and holding in common the job title 'social worker'. Collectively, social workers were responsible for delivering a wide array of personal social services in the field. And so from 'a relatively small scale enterprise' social work had 'become big business' (Goldberg and Warburton 1979, p.1). The observations and results of these investigations helped describe how the distribution of social workers and their work was settling down and shaping up.

Writing in the area ranges from relatively factual reports on the scope and pattern of social work practice through to more speculative accounts about the reasons for such distributions in social work's manpower. Others go a stage further and comment on the rights and wrongs of the situation. The literature generated by the studies can be considered under four main headings: (1) Social workers: numbers and settings; (2) The distribution of social workers and their work: research observations and analyses; (3) Explanations of the distribution of social workers and their work; (4) Evaluations of the distribution of social workers and their work. The rest of this chapter looks at the first two. Chapter 3 reviews some of the explanations and evaluations of the distribution of workers that currently exist.

SOCIAL WORKERS: NUMBERS AND SETTINGS

Throughout the 1970s there was a regular increase in the number of field social workers employed by local authority SSDs. Between 1972 and 1975 there was a 28 per cent increase in the number of social workers employed and a massive 144 per cent increase in the employment of social work assistants (DHSS,

S/F 76/1 1976). Most people who work for local authority SSDs are not, in fact, social workers. For example, in England for the year 1982, out of 199,529 whole time equivalent people employed by local authority Social Services Departments, only 18,140 (9.1 per cent) were fieldworkers (Health and PSS Statistics 1982/DHSS). The remaining numbers are made up of such people as managers, residential staff, administrators and home help organisers. The 18,140 fieldworkers were to be found in 108 local authorities, including London and the metropolitan counties, giving an average of 168 field social workers and social work assistants per authority. However, in practice there is considerable variation in the number of fieldworkers employed by different authorities. A small urban authority such as Solihull had 53 social workers and social work assistants in 1981. Much larger departments might employ hundreds of fieldstaff. Essex, for example, recorded over 450 field social workers in 1981, while Liverpool had 359 similarly employed (DHSS LA Social Services Statistics 1981, S/F 82/1).

THE DISTRIBUTION OF SOCIAL WORKERS AND THEIR WORK: RESEARCH OBSERVATIONS AND ANALYSES

There have been a small number of major studies and an array of smaller enquiries which between them have generated considerable information on the characteristics of social workers and their activities in SSDs. Evidence on the actual distribution of fieldworkers has not necessarily been their prime aim. However, an examination of their findings allows a sketch to be pieced together. Particular reference is made to four studies which have yielded material germane to the enquiry.

Goldberg and her colleagues took a very detailed look at what social workers were doing in one area team in Southampton (Goldberg and Fruin 1976; Goldberg et al. 1977 and 1978). The team comprised the equivalent of 20 full time social workers and social work assistants whose work was recorded between 1 February 1975 and 31 January 1976. The data produced was extensive and quantitative as it related to the one team.

Stevenson and Parsloe (1978) and their team of researchers observed a wide range of workers in social services and social work departments throughout England, Wales, Northern Ireland and Scotland. As well as other social services personnel, about 200 social workers and social work assistants took part in the study. They were drawn from 31 area and sub-area teams throughout eight local authorities. Participant observation and unstructured interviews were the main research methods employed although there was some statistical work undertaken on students and social workers after training. Most of the evidence is recorded in descriptive, qualitative and anecdotal form, giving an impressionistic account of social work in area teams as it appeared to the researchers in the mid-1970s,

Holme and Maizels (1978) sampled a large number of field-workers on a nationwide basis. There respondents were contacted by postal questionnaire. 1,529 local authority social workers and social work assistants were approached. 829 replied giving a response rate of 54%. Although the main aim was to examine the use that social workers and probation officers made of volunteers, in order to advance their purpose the researchers obtained and reported a considerable amount of statistical information about social workers and their caseloads.

In 1979, I surveyed 285 social workers and social work assistants from three SSDs, two of which were located in metropolitan boroughs and one in a county authority. Using a questionnaire, information was obtained on the composition of individual caseloads along with biographical details for each fieldworker. The results are reported in this chapter.

The studies can be examined in two particular areas: (i) the bias present in caseloads, and (ii) the distribution of client groups amongst different types of fieldworker.

(i) The bias present in caseloads

Throughout the course of a year, one or two thousand clients might be seen by a typical area team. In the Southampton studies, the area's intake team recorded the main problems as given at first referral over a calendar year. 2,019 referrals were received (Goldberg et al. 1977). Nearly a third of the main problems were associated with physical disability, illness or ageing (30%). 'Financial and material problems (17%), delinquency (15%) and other child behaviour and family relationship problems (14%) constituted the other large groups.' (p.262) Mental and emotional disorders were present in 7% of the initial referrals. If a social worker's own workload over a period of time reflects the general mix of client groupings found within the team, that social worker could be described as having a mixed or 'generic' caseload.

In most studies, caseloads are observed and analysed mainly in terms of the major client groupings. Though not particularly sophisticated, this classification reflects the way both local and central government departments record and understand fieldworkers' caseloads. It is also the way most fieldworkers describe and perceive their work. Nearly all the informal specialisation found in the studies directed by Stevenson and Parsloe 'was concerned with client groups, conventionally defined, or with subgroups, such as adolescents' (1978, p.144).

Holme and Maizels' study revealed that a substantial number of social workers had caseloads which entirely excluded certain client groups. This picture was confirmed by Stevenson and Parsloe. 'In every team we visited we were told of some, and often a majority, of members who had moved towards a bias towards certain types of client'. (p.172) It seemed that most social workers welcomed what was termed a 'bias within genericism', and a few appeared to have totally specialised caseloads.

Holme and Maizels (1978) also distinguished caseloads according to the direction of their bias. This was indicated by the extent to which particular client groups represented 40% or more of a social worker's caseload, where the term social worker included social work assistants and trainees but excluded occupational therapists and home help organisers. Even though they employ eight different kinds of client group (thereby reducing the chances of any social worker achieving a 40% presence of a particular client group in their caseload), the authors show that 61% of social workers display a modest bias in their caseload. Commenting on these results the authors say that 'Where caseload bias occurs ... it is more likely to be towards children and, to a lesser extent, physically handicapped clients, than towards any other group', though many of those registered as physically handicapped are also aged over 65 (p.130).

In my own study, 199 fieldworkers had caseloads which had a _marked bias_ (70% and over) towards work with a particular client group. Table 2:1 reports in detail the number of caseloads which had such a marked bias as well as the number in which no one client group assumed more than a 70% presence in the total caseload.

Table 2:1
Extent of biased baseloads

Client Group Category	Proportion of all fieldworkers with biased baseloads (that is caseloads which have one client category comprising more than 70% of the total number of that fieldworker's cases		
	Type of authority		
	County	Metropolitan	Total
	%	%	%
Children and their families	29	63	43
Mentally ill and mentally handicapped	9	0	5
Elderly and physically handicapped	27	15	22
(Proportion with no marked caseload bias	35	23	30)
Total	100	101	100
N =	156	129	285

A number of points emerge from Table 2:1: (i) the majority of fieldworkers (70%) had a marked bias in their caseload; (ii) 43% of all fieldworkers had caseloads which were markedly biased towards working with children and their families; (iii) 22% of fieldworkers had a marked bias in their caseload towards the elderly and physically handicapped; (iv) only 5% of all fieldworkers achieved a caseload biased towards the mentally ill and handicapped; (v) this left 30% of all fieldworkers with a caseload showing no marked bias, suggesting that their caseloads could be described as 'generic'. Three types of fieldworker might be more likely to build up generic caseloads. First, there are those social workers with less than two years' experience. Second, there are 'intake' social workers who specialised in duty and short term work. They handled all incoming work and this was reflected in the more generic composition of their caseload. 50% of intake workers had caseloads with a marked bias split equally in the direction of child care and work with the old and disabled. Third, rural social workers tended to have more mixed caseloads. It is often the practice in area teams which cover large areas for social workers to operate on a 'patch' system. In this arrangement, each social worker is responsible for all the work generated within a small patch of the overall area. If intake workers and rurally based workers are removed from the sample, 79% of the remaining fieldworkers had a marked bias in their caseload towards a particular client group.

Table 2:1 shows that certain client groups tended to be concentrated in particular caseloads. The significant number of departures from the generic condition indicates that a considerable degree of differentiation existed among the ranks of the local authority fieldworkers. It appeared that most fieldworkers were not doing most things. Most fieldworkers were only doing some things, and different things at that.

In general, these empirical forays into the life of SSDs show that different types of client group have become relatively concentrated in the hands of different fieldworkers. As Stevenson points out, bias and specialisation can arise in a number of ways (Stevenson 1981 passim). Informal specialisation amongst team members as well as formal specialisation as a result of deliberate area or departmental policy both result in different sorts of work going in different directions within the area team. But on the whole the impression gained by researchers was 'that specialisms, both formal and informal, did not, in general, arise from deliberate policies or decisions taken at senior level. Their preservation and development seemed more reactive than innovative.' (Stevenson and Parsloe 1978, p.198)

(ii) The distribution of client groups amongst different types of fieldworker

Fieldworkers in local authority area teams may vary in a number of ways. There are social workers who may or may not be professionally qualified (holders of the Certificate of Qualification in Social Work). There are social work assistants (sometimes known as welfare assistants) who more often than not 'assist' no-one but are responsible for their own caseloads (Stevenson and Parsloe 1978, p.137). Fieldworkers will differ in age, sex, education, experience and length of service. Different amalgams of these characteristics produce different 'types' of fieldworker.

Three particular associations of worker and client group types can be recognised in the literature:

(1) Work with children and their families, and in particular 'statutory work' (by which is meant children 'at risk', 'in

care' or under formal supervision) appeared to be in the hands
mainly of qualified or experienced social workers (Stevenson
and Parsloe 1978, pp.60, 388-89). For example Goldberg et al.
(1978, pp.269 and 273) found that 72% of the long term work
with children in care and 64% of work with child behaviour and
family relationship problems was being carried out by
qualified social workers in the Southampton area.

(2) In contrast, fieldwork with old people and to some extent
the disabled was being handled by either unqualified social
workers or more likely, social work assistants. One respondent
in Stevenson and Parsloe's study explained that 'The social
work assistants in our district provide the social work service
to the elderly ... In fact, they are the social workers for
the elderly.' (p.140). Social work assistants also tend to
have larger caseloads than social workers (Holme and Maizels
1978, pp.130, 134-5; Stevenson and Parsloe 1978, p.139).
Moreover Holme and Maizels (1978, p.135) noticed that the
smaller the caseload the larger the representation of child
care cases, while the larger the caseload the larger the
representation of the old and disabled.

Most social work assistants appear to be women (Holme and
Maizels 1978; Stevenson and Parsloe 1978), and thus by
implication most social work with old people is being done by
women. There is little detailed information on the age
structure of social work assistants, but as Stevenson and
Parsloe coyly (and oddly for researchers) put it 'We did not
ask the assistants interviewed to disclose their age but', they
add, less chivalrously, 'our observations tell us that all but
three could be described as middle-aged or over.' (p.137).

More generally, the conclusion from my own work was that
whereas only 6% of all men had a caseload bias towards the old
and disabled, 17% of women achieved such a bias. Thus, 82% of
all caseloads carried by social workers and having a marked
bias to work with the old and disabled were held by women.
Throughout the fieldworker range, whether it was social workers
who were qualified or graduates, unqualified or non-graduates,
women were always proportionately more likely to have had caseloads which showed a marked bias towards the old and disabled
than men. In my survey there were 4,873 cases involving work
with the old and disabled. 3,753 of these cases (77%) were
carried by women, a statistically highly significant proportion (DF = 1, x^2 = 357, p = <0.001).

(3) Relative to work with children and old people, there are
proportionately fewer cases concerning the mentally ill and
mentally handicapped. Therefore specialisation was altogether
less common in the direction of 'mental health' work in area

teams (Stevenson and Parsloe 1978, pp.107, 172). However when bias or specialisation did occur, qualified social workers appeared more likely to be managing cases involving mental illness than mental handicap, while unqualified social workers and social work assistants were more likely to be working with the mentally handicapped than the mentally ill (Goldberg and Warburton 1979, p.115). Evidence on sex distribution comes from the pre-Seebohm mental health departments where men were more prevalent in work with mental illness than women (see Walton 1975, pp.232-33).

The relationship between the type of worker and the composition of that worker's caseload can also be analysed. The 285 fieldworkers and their caseloads from my own survey were examined in this way. Table 2:2 shows that 74% of qualified social workers had a marked bias in their caseloads with the majority (59%) expressing that bias towards work with children and their families. Proportionately few had a bias towards work with the old and handicapped (9%) or mental health cases (6%). A large proportion of social work assistants (97%) possessed caseloads which had a bias, but this was almost exclusively towards work with the old and disabled (91%). Fewer unqualified social workers had a biased caseload (53%). When bias did occur it was as likely to be towards the old and disabled (22%) as towards work with children and their families (27%).

It was also found that whether or not the fieldworker held a first degree affected the composition of the caseload, but only if the worker was also qualified. 84% of qualified graduate social workers had caseloads which had a marked bias with this bias going almost entirely towards work with children and their families (82%). Qualified social workers who were not graduates were less liable to have a marked caseload bias (68%), with fewer going in the direction of child care work (43%) and proportionately more towards the old and disabled (14%) and mental health cases (11%). Indeed of the few social workers (N = 14) who displayed a marked bias towards mental health work, the majority (N = 10) were qualified but non-graduates (71%).

In order to explore matters further, I approached two more SSDs and obtained broad data on the grading levels of all fieldworkers and the composition of their caseloads. Table 2:3 describes the results. It can be seen that Level 3 workers handled nearly half of all child care and family work in the departments, but only 15% of work with the elderly. Mental health work was an intermediate speciality with nearly half the departments' Level 2 workers practising in this field. The elderly and disabled were concentrated on the caseloads of the lowest grade workers.

Table 2:2

Caseload composition and fieldworker training

Type of Fieldworker	Number of fieldworkers with more than 70% (marked bias) of caseload composed of one client group				Number of fieldworkers in which no client group achieved 70% presence in caseload	Total number of fieldworkers
	Client Groups (with row %)					
	Children and their families	Mental Health	Elderly and Disabled	Total		
Qualified social workers	95 (59%)	10 (6%)	14 (9%)	119 (74%)	41 (26%)	160 (100%)
Unqualified social workers	25 (27%)	4 (4%)	20 (22%)	49 (53%)	44 (47%)	93 (100%)
Social work assistants	2 (6%)	0 (0%)	29 (91%)	31 (97%)	1 (3%)	32 (100%)
Total	122	14	63	199	86	285

$x^2 = 128.8$ df = 6 p = <0.001

$x^2 = 39.4$ df = 3 p = <0.001

(for qualified and unqualified workers only)

Table 2:3

Caseload composition and level of social worker

Number of cases (held by 298 fieldworkers)

Type of case	Level of social worker			Social Work Assistants	Total
	Level 3	Level 2	Level 1		
Children and their families	2,649 (47%)	2,142 (38%)	676 (12%)	169 (3%)	5,636 (100%)
Mental health	713 (34%)	1,028 (49%)	294 (14%)	63 (3%)	2,098 (100%)
Old and physically handicapped	844 (15%)	1,914 (34%)	2,027 (36%)	845 (15%)	5,630 (100%)
Total	4,206 (31%)	5,084 (38%)	2,997 (22%)	1,077 (8%)	13,364 (100%)

df = 6 x^2 = 2,396.1   p = <0.001

CONCLUSION

Bebbington and Davies (1979) examined relationships between social workers and client numbers in 79 out of 108 English SSDs. They found that the number of child care cases most powerfully determined the number of workers in a department. For example, the more children in the care of the local authority, the more fieldworkers were employed, 'and a difference of seventeen children in care tends on average to be accompanied by an additional basic grade worker' (p.95). Child care workers were most likely to be qualified and experienced. Further, the number of elderly persons potentially requiring social work inputs has a substantial influence on the number of social work assistants employed, though the numbers of elderly has negligible effect on the overall number of basic grade workers and senior staff (p.95).

In all surveys the distribution of work and workers is seen to be a function of the characteristics of the client group and the characteristics of the worker. Therefore in answer to the question 'who is working with whom?', it appears that certain types of worker are more likely to be working with particular kinds of client group than others. The fieldworker's job designation, qualifications, sex and experience all have a bearing on the proportion which each client group is likely to achieve in an individual's caseload. To this extent the work and workers in area teams are clearly differentiated. Indeed, the stratification of both work and workers emerges as the major observation of the surveys reviewed.

3 Ditching the dirty work

EXPLANATIONS OF THE DISTRIBUTION OF SOCIAL WORKERS AND THEIR CLIENTS

Observations concerning the distribution of social workers amongst the various client groups have received little in the way of systematic explanation. If the pattern of fieldworker deployment is not taken to be self-explanatory then explanations tend to be offered in passing, often as a preface to more evaluative comments about what should be the case in manpower distribution in the personal social services. When explanations do occur, they arise on an ad hoc basis. They appear like the tips of an iceberg, superficial accounts with no attempt to connect each surface manifestation at some deeper level involving the nature of the work and its overall organisation. Explanations address themselves to one or other of the two main survey observations: explanations of specialisation and bias in the caseloads of fieldworkers and explanations of the selective distribution of client groups amongst different kinds of fieldworkers.

EXPLANATIONS OF SPECIALISATION AND BIAS IN THE CASELOADS OF FIELDWORKERS

The concentration of specific types of work in the caseloads of individual workers is accounted for in a number of ways. These may be reduced to give five types of explanation:

(1) Volume of work

There are differences in the volume of work for each client group that each area team has to handle. This favours the appearance of some client groups on caseloads more than others (Goldberg et al. 1977, p.262; Holme and Maizels 1978). As work with the old and frail and children and their families predominates, most fieldworkers, particularly those in longer term work, are likely in the absence of other selection mechanisms operating, to have the bulk of their work made up of these two client groupings. The first priority, note Goldberg et al. (1977), appears to be the provision of 'protective services for the most vulnerable groups - the very young and helpless and the very old and disabled. These two groups emerged as the most likely to receive long-term care.' (p.262).

(2) Work preferences

The majority of social workers express a preference for some client groups and areas of work over others. It has been explained how social workers and their work are categorised, and how these categories provide a basis on which to recognise the differentiation of both work and workers. Each type of worker and client group category is also eligible for evaluation. Easthope (1975, p.62) has written that (i) when phenomena are categorised and (ii) those categories are evaluated, the result is a hierarchy. Although there are slight differences in detail between studies, the most preferred types of work involved children and their families (generally over 60% of fieldworkers in most of the studies). The least preferred groups included the elderly, disabled and mentally handicapped (between 10 and 30%) (Holme and Maizels 1978, pp.142-46; Neill et al. 1976; Rees 1978, pp.49 and 50; Stevenson and Parsloe 1978, pp.367-68). Even during training social work students appear to have developed clear preferences. According to Stevenson and Parsloe (1978), 88% of their sample of students would like to work with children but only 34%, 31% and 28% welcomed the prospect of working with the mentally handicapped, sick and disabled and elderly respectively (p.367).

The 285 fieldworkers in my study of three SSDs were asked with which client group or problem area they would prefer to work. Of those expressing a preference, 98% stated a client group rather than a problem area as their preference. The replies were categoriesed in terms of the three main client groups. 82% of all fieldworkers had a preference for working with a particular client group.

Of all the respondents, 50% preferred work within the category 'work with children and their families'. This figure increased to 60% if only qualified social workers were considered. 17% of fieldworkers expressed a preference for working with the old and physically handicapped. The majority of these (65%) were untrained workers. This meant that whereas 26% of untrained workers were prepared to express a preference for work with the old and disabled, only 16% of qualified workers were willing to do the same. 14% of fieldworkers preferred work involving the mentally ill or the mentally handicapped. Of those fieldworkers expressing a preference, 65% (N = 151) said that they would like to work <u>exclusively</u> in that area.

This left 18% of fieldworkers with no particular area of work preferred. Many in this group were relative newcomers to social work, often with less than two years experience of SSDs. As time in social services increases, the desire to work generically appears to diminish. For example, whereas 32% of fieldworkers with less than two years experience in social work held no preference for one particular client group, this figure dropped significantly to 13% for those with four years experience or more ($p = <0.01$).

Holme and Maizels further demonstrate that preferences, with some exceptions, tend to be satisfied in practice: 'The degree of correspondence between social workers' preferences for particular client groups, and the presence of these groups in their caseloads, is extremely high.' (pp.145-6). The existence of preferences and their satisfaction could account for the presence of bias in caseloads. However the authors qualify their findings with two additional comments. First, 'perhaps social workers come to like what they do' (p.146). And second, satisfaction of preferences is not uniform and is related to job designation, being highest for social workers (81.2% correspondence) and lowest for social work assistants (68.4% correspondence).

I found that out of the 285 fieldworkers surveyed, 86 had worked in a pre-1971 department and had survived the Seebohm disturbance and the subsequent years as fieldworkers. In general, if the fieldworker had worked in a children's, welfare or mental health department, the past association influenced both the current caseload and area of work preferred. Experience in a pre-Seebohm department encourages the social worker to maintain interest in the 'old' client group. 84% of ex-child care officers still preferred to work with children and their families. Equally high, 81% of ex-mental welfare

officers preferred to work in the area of mental health. The
only likely erosion of loyalty was amongst the ex-welfare
officers, although even here, 47% still would like to be
involved with the old and physically handicapped.

(3) Client group priorities

In many SSDs certain problems and client groups are given
priority, either formally or informally. The granting of
priority may take several forms. Certain cases, particularly
child care work, may receive swift allocation and departmental
policy may require the fieldworker to give a prompt response
(e.g. Rees 1978, p.46; Stevenson and Parsloe 1978, p.60).
'The highest priority of all departments which we visited',
write Stevenson and Parsloe, 'was child care' (1978, p.173).
And as one social worker put it, 'first child care, second
mental health, third the elderly'. The authors believe that
the reason for this 'no doubt reflects ... national priorities
and is reinforced by the media, especially when a tragedy
occurs' (p.169). Child care issues have generated more legislation of a more detailed kind than any other client group.
Priorities, explains Hey (1979) are 'emphasised by the degree
of specificity in legislation and statutory instruments
relating to child and family care, as compared with the lack of
specificity about protection and standards in relation to adult
groups, no matter what problems they face' (p.178).

   Reports on the amount of time, the level of service and the
intensity of involvement also indicate that child care is
favoured with greater levels of input than work involving old
people and the handicapped (Goldberg eg al. 1978; Ward, Fogg
and Pottage 1973).

   Many SSDs use systems of 'caseload weightings' which assume
that certain types of work entail more time and effort than
others. This allows social workers to hold proportionately
fewer cases which carry a heavy weighting with the corres-
ponding expectation that they would be able to deal with a
greater number of lightly weighted cases. Although there is a
certain circularity in the logic of this system, the net effect
is for area teams to maintain and retain work about which the
department is alert and sensitive. Weighting systems generally
favour child care work, particularly with young children.

(4) Pre-Seebohm experience

Certainly in the years immediately after the formation of SSDs
the composition of the caseloads of social workers was
determined by their pre-Seebohm experience. 'Older staff felt
secure with previous specialism', records Rees (1978, p.49).

There was a reluctance to take on new areas of work (Hey 1979, p.175; Neill et al. 1973). In Goldberg's Southampton studies most work with the long-term elderly was 'carried by two ex-welfare officers' (Goldberg et al. 1978, p.259), while Stevenson and Parsloe observed that many social workers said they felt ill-equipped to deal with the mentally ill; the exceptions included social workers who 'had nursed in the local psychiatric hospital' or 'others who had been mental welfare officers ... before reorganisation'. (1978, p.107).

I also found that experience in a pre-Seebohm department had a significant influence on the current composition of the worker's caseload. There was some erosion of loyalty to past client groups in the case of ex-welfare and mental welfare workers, hinting at the seductive capacities of child care work. Even so, a large proportion of the 86 pre-Seebohm workers retained caseloads heavily biased towards their old client group. 81% of social workers who had previously worked in a children's department now had a caseload with a marked bias towards work with 'children and their families'. 47% of ex-welfare officers still had their work biased in a 'welfare' direction, although for all other social workers only 9% achieved a bias towards work with the old and physically handicapped. And in spite of the low numbers overall, 29% of those who had worked in a mental health department still had a caseload made up predominantly of the mentally ill and mentally handicapped, compared to only 4% of all other field-workers. With only a little exaggeration, it is possible to say that a large number of fieldworkers negotiated reorganisation relatively intact, at least as far as their caseloads were concerned, remaining as either child care, mental welfare or welfare officers.

(5) Managing the work

The range of knowledge and personal ability required to cope sensibly with the full range of field social services work is too great for most individuals (Hey 1979, pp.174-75; Mattinson and Sinclair 1979, pp.256-65; Neill et al. 1976; Stevenson 1968). 'From the sheer necessity of having to divide social work tasks into manageable packages', client group specialisms will continue to exist believes Vickery (Social Work Today 26.7.73, p.265) lest there arise a feeling of 'impotence' and being a 'jack-of-all-trades and master of none' (Goldberg and Warburton 1979, p.15). The need to specialise, in the words of one social worker, is to 'narrow my knowledge and be effective' (Neill et al. 1976, p.11) echoing a reflection offered by Titmuss (1976, p.41) that 'it is a great comfort to acquire 'one small allotment in the vastness of the knowable' where one feels a little more at home and in peace; a little more professionally secure'.

EXPLANATIONS OF THE DIFFERENTIAL DISTRIBUTION OF CLIENT GROUPS AMONGST FIELDWORKERS

(1) Historical inertia

The new SSDs did not represent an abrupt break with the old departments and past practices. Personnel and styles of work carried over and informed many aspects of post-Seebohm life, including the kind of worker most likely to be working with particular client groups. In the first years after reorganisation there was a 'possessiveness' towards old specialisms (Neill et al. 1973, p.460) which helped maintain the tradition of certain kinds of staff working with particular client groups.

The child care services had always managed to attract qualified staff and graduates in respectable numbers. For example, in 1967, 53% of field officers in children's departments either were qualified or held a degree compared to only 28% of mental health officers and 18% of welfare officers (Seebohm Report 1968, Appendix M).

Looking back over twenty five years or more of social work, it seemed to Younghusband (1978, pp.239-49) that not much had changed in terms of the levels of staff training and the status of the work (between the young, the mentally ill, the handicapped and the old). She gives the example of mental health workers who in 1951 were 'gravely concerned ... by the dearth of trained and experienced workers ... in mental deficiency work' which was the 'Cinderella' of the social services (Younghusband 1951, pp.88-89). This state of affairs was echoed later by Julia's recollection that in 1960 'it was traditional ... for trained social workers to work with the mentally ill and for the work with the mentally handicapped to be carried out by less skilled staff' (Julia 1978, p.7).

(2) Complexity and skill

Accounting for the distribution of fieldworkers in terms of the skills possessed and the complexity of work faced is the most common explanation. Generally the explanation contains the following sequence of reasoning: Child care and family work is more complex, difficult and important than work with other client groups, particularly the disabled, elderly and mentally handicapped which are considered 'less weighty', 'often practical' and very often just 'routine' (Stevenson and Parsloe 1978, pp.141-42; also see Black et al. 1983, p.224). Qualified social workers have the training and skills to deal with complex and difficult work whereas unqualified social workers and social work assistants are better suited to dealing with 'straightforward' cases (Stevenson and Parsloe 1978, p.142). The distribution of work and workers is based on the differences in the types of response demanded by different client groups and in the different abilities of social workers to supply those responses.

Evidence to support this line of explanation is drawn from studies which have examined (i) the problems, tasks and activities (the characteristics of the work) associated with different client groups, and (ii) the responses and activities identified with different types of fieldworker.

<u>The characteristics of the work associated with different client groups</u>. In broad terms, work with the old and handicapped involves mainly surveillance and organising practical services while child care and family difficulties witness the provision of skilled 'casework' services and 'help in coping with emotional and relationship problems' (Brearley in Booth et al. (eds) 1980, p.41; Goldberg and Warburton 1979, p.12). Earlier work by the National Institute of Social Work showed similar differences; social workers gave more time and offered different types of service to child care cases than to clients who were old and disabled (Boardman 1977; Carver and Edwards 1972).

In detail, Goldberg et al's (1978) work described clients who were having problems with their child's behaviour and family relationships. These received intensive social work help (5.4 contacts/quarter). Outside agencies were involved in over four-fifths of these cases (p.274). Problem solving was attempted in half of the cases and was considered the most important activity in over a quarter, higher proportions than in any other client group. And since most of the target problems were related to behaviour, attitudes and relationships, 'the major change area, where contemplated at all, was that of behaviour and attitudes (35%) - far above the proportion for all client groups' (p.275). Corby (1982, pp.625-26) records that personal and interpersonal problems were particularly predominant in work with children and their families.

Child care cases 'were considered to be "more difficult"' by Stevenson and Parsloe's (1978, p.173) respondents, 'and this led to their being allocated to qualified and experienced workers'. Indeed the suggestion is that social workers seek out work which allows the exercise of their casework skills and these are most readily identified and sought in child care work

(Rees 1978, p.49). According to Prottas (1979, p.118) welfare workers generally single out 'clients who represent a professional opportunity'. Wilkes (1981) enlarges on this theme arguing that as social workers turn increasingly to goal-oriented methods in their casework, 'there is considerable danger ... that high priority is granted to areas of work in which effective results are easily demonstrable. In consequence, work with undervalued groups such as the elderly, the dying, or the physically or mentally handicapped, for whom 'remedies' cannot be easily prescribed ... is relegated to a secondary position' (back cover).

Although there appear to be far fewer cases involving problems of mental and emotional disorder, in Goldberg et al's (1978) studies, they received the most intensive contact (8.1/quarter) (p.280). McAuley et al. (1983) studied social work tasks in an acute psychiatric in-patient unit. Their results compare with Goldberg et al's. The most outstanding finding was that 55% of all subjects (N = 120) had family relationship problems followed by 35% experiencing loneliness and isolation. 'As in all the other long-term cases', continue Goldberg et al. (1978, p.281), 'check up review visiting (66%) was recorded in the majority of cases', with 'sustaining and nurturing' occurring as the second most common activity. There was a high incidence of contact with outside agencies, although the general 'impression' was one of social workers 'holding a watching brief' (p.281).

With the mentally handicapped and elderly, review visits and mobilising resources featured as the most common activities in all studies (Black et al. 1983; Corby 1982, p.626; Crosbie 1983; Goldberg et al. 1978). For the long-term elderly, plans generally entailed merely the 'continuance of domiciliary services' and 'occasional surveillance' (Goldberg et al. 1978, p.262), 'rather than involving ongoing relationships with clients' (Satyamurti 1981, p.11). This could hardly be otherwise, believes Satyamurti (p.11), given that in her study of the pre-Seebohm departments, welfare workers carried caseloads of over a hundred while child care officers averaged only forty. The routine and material help normally given to these groups was generally felt to be 'something which could probably be carried out by a welfare assistant (Rees 1948, p.56). Carter (quoted in Crosbie 1983, p.123), in fact, has cast doubt on the need to employ large numbers of qualified social workers for work with the elderly. Although seen as light relief in small measure by some social workers, in the replies received by Rees (1978, pp.56 and 141), social work with old people was seen as dull and unrewarding. In his review of social workers' attitudes to the elderly Harris (1979, p.38) concluded that 'They are seen as unchallenging because they require practical services and unresponsive because they are unamenable to social workers' attempts to change them'.

The characteristics of the work associated with different types of worker. Rather than start from an analysis of tasks generated by different client groups and match the appropriate fieldworker, the reverse process is also possible. Here, the job or roles of the fieldworker are analysed to see what he or she is doing and the perceived needs of the case are matched to the worker. Such an approach has been taken by Jeans, making use of American work which examines the tasks and roles present in personal social services work (Jeans 1978).

Jean's 'first impression is of a basic similarity between the work undertaken by the various categories of workers studied' (p.38). The subtle differences noticed included a slight loading towards the more 'therapeutic' kinds of activity on the part of qualified and experienced workers while 'care giving' and 'supportive work' was more frequently offered by workers who, though experienced, were unqualified. And although '"behaviour changing" seems to be the province of the professionally qualified staff', in fact it hardly featured in their practice (p.40). The main point was 'to test the feasibility of using "functional roles" as a useful means of describing team field social work activity with a view to linking required skills and knowledge with the demands of different forms of daily practice in different settings' (p.20). This sounds suspiciously like saying that evidence about what different social workers do in practice is an indication of what they should and would do in future practice. Even so, the approach provides information about what different types of social workers do with the implicit suggestion that those whose role proclivities match what is believed to be present and required in a particular client group should be allocated work of that kind. In this fashion, social work assistants with care and support featuring strongly in their practice should find themselves working with the elderly who seem to need these very things, while qualified social workers with hints of therapeutic and 'teaching' skills are better equipped to tackle child care and family work.

(3) Professional manoeuvres: ditching the dirty work

Scott (1970), enlarging on some of the earlier insights offered by Goffman, writes:

> Throughout history, the mentally ill, the crippled, the mentally retarded, the maimed, the poor, and others who were similarly stigmatised as morally inferior have

occupied an unenviable status in most societies of the world. Traditionally, such persons have been viewed as helpless dependents, incapable of mastering the elementary skills essential for engaging in productive social and economic activities. Mingled with these ideas were certain imputations about moral culpability.

In discussing stigma, Pinker (1971) also recognises that different values are placed on individuals depending on the extent to which they are economically dependent on the efforts of others. Value is also judged in terms of the future economic potential of the individual and the group to which he belongs. The elderly and the mentally handicapped, for example, are seen as having a high dependence and low productive potential and are therefore a highly stigmatised group. Children, though dependent, have the capacity to become future producers, and throughout the welfare services they are a group much less likely to suffer heavy stigmatisation.

This hierarchy of worth is often mirrored in the relative value of resources made available to each of the groups, and further reflects the status of those particular members of professional occupations who work with these categories. Low status medicine and nursing, for example, is to be found in the fields of geriatrics and mental retardation, and not paediatrics or obstetrics.

Closely associated with the development of hierarchies within occupations are the phenomena of professionalisation and 'dirty work'. Work can be dirty in several ways (Hughes 1958, p.49). It may be physically disgusting. Dustbinmen, those who attend to the incontinent elderly, and sewer workers have physically odious jobs. The work may be morally dubious and degrading, as with criminals and prostitutes. It may be work which involves carrying out what other people would rather not do.

However, to caste some jobs as dirty, whether physically, morally or symbolically, reflects what is and what is not valued in society. To relegate and degrade certain types of work, to put them outside the normal ranges of propriety and regard them as somehow deviant, leaves other jobs in a more favourable light and better rewarded. Dirty work is that which 'in some way goes counter to the more heroic of our moral conceptions' (Hughes 1958, pp.49-50), where our moral conceptions are derived from the values of the society in which we live. Dirty work includes those activities which have to be done but are nevertheless distasteful in the doing, and those which ought not to be done but unfortunately seem unavoidable.

The notion of dirty work also applies equally to jobs in

which people are the objects of attention. They may not be
physically pleasant. People can be dirty, unwholesome and
physically disgusting. 'People-workers' can also do personally
and socially unpleasant things such as remove individuals to
psychiatric hospital against their wishes or keep people
locked up in prison. Distastefulness in jobs like prison
officer, doss-house keeper and psychiatric nurse with the
confused elderly can be seen to combine two 'dirty' elements -
(i) <u>what</u> is being done, and (ii) <u>with whom</u> it is being done.
For many of those who work in the personal social services,
these twin elements, either by their relative presence or
absence, determine what is seen to be attractive or unpleasant.

However, to gauge whether work is to be recognised as clean
or dirty, valuable or unimportant, reference has to be made to
some set of standards. It is the presence of norms or
standards that allows work to be viewed unequally. And
inequalities in the value placed on the work to be done act as
a measure by which rising occupations might gauge what is
worth pursuing and what is best left for others to do.

Choosing your work is like choosing your friends; you may be
judged by the company you keep. Occupations like social work,
nursing and teaching have always been rather sensitive about
their image. In order to correct what the incumbents of these
jobs see as misconceptions about what they do, the worthy and
more complex parts of their work are emphasised, little mention
being made of activities of a more humble kind. Teachers are
to be understood in terms of their pedagogic skills and the
hard won techniques that promote learning in reluctant minds
and not as people who tie up shoe laces or act as glorified
child-minders. Nurses are the technicians of the ward, skilled
in reading medical instruments and administering drugs. Little
is said about the making of beds or following a doctor's
instructions. Difficult casework and delicate decision making
in risky cases of child abuse are likely to be emphasised by
social workers and not the half hour spent in listening to an
upset old lady explain that she has lost her pension book and
there is nothing in the house to eat.

From choosing not to talk about less prestigious aspects of
the work in order to polish up the job's appearance, it is but
a short step not to do it at all. In that way there is not the
bother of trying to play down the unglamorous side of the work.
The job can then be seen as legitimate, honourable and
respectable.

The privilege of opting out of less elevated practices is, of
course, not open to everyone. Someone has to do the dirty work.
But only some people are able to have their choices realised.

As there is large scale agreement about which are the desirable things to be doing, there is a general movement into these areas by those workers who have the ability to practise what they prefer.

Hughes (1958) observes that any occupational group that wishes to enhance its status must choose its work carefully. Areas of work which are physically or morally 'dirty', which are not highly valued by society and regarded as menial are not likely to bring professional status to those who practise such jobs. In fact the 'delegation of dirty work is ... a part of the process of occupational mobility' (p.52) and 'ranking has something to do with the relative cleanliness of functions performed' (p.72). Any group which wishes to improve its professional standing does well if it can delegate the more lowly, routine and 'dirty' aspects of its work to other workers lower down in the occupational hierarchy.

Carpenter (1977) on nursing since the 1966 Salmon reorganisation, records how the higher paid and higher status jobs in nursing have improved and are now associated with the 'clean' end of the job, particularly the administrative and management side of nursing. At the dirty end of the job's spectrum, much of the basic physical care of the patient (removing soiled sheets, washing patients and the like) has been delegated to nursing auxiliaries.

The process of differentiation and stratification that seems to be occurring in the area teams of SSDs might be discussed in the light of these concepts. The 'clean' end of the job is the work associated with lowly stigmatised, potentially productive, aesthetically pleasing category of 'children and their families'. If an occupation, such as social work, wished to increase its status, this would be the right area on which to concentrate. But in order to achieve this specialisation, the less attractive groups, both physically and productively, would need to be handled by other workers. The results of the surveys show the elderly and physically handicapped as the groups most likely to be receiving help from social work assistants and low status social workers, leaving the higher status social workers to concentrate their efforts on the more prestigious client categories.

Extracting work which is well regarded and practising in clean, well-favoured areas is an effective way of revising and upgrading conceptions of the job and those who do it. In contrast, those members who have to endure their clientele, have no say in their selection, and, in effect, receive other people's rejects, are the dirty workers. Dirty workers underpin respectable practice.

When dirty work is delegated, we have what McKinlay (1975) refers to as 'creaming'. Clients are selected on the basis of what they can do for the practitioner. The elimination of cases which are perceived as likely to jeopardise the realisation of certain professional goals promotes occupational mobility. According to this argument, it would seem that the status of any profession may be a function of the status of its clientele. 'Indeed', McKinlay (1975, p.363) goes on to say, 'because the designation "professional" is perhaps more dependent on societal reaction than on the intrinsic character of tasks or training, we may find certain groups sensitive to association with people or tasks which would question the applicability of the label.'

The net effect of 'professionalisation' is to downgrade certain sorts of work which are then ripe for delegation. This ditched work is devoid of occupational potential. The cleansing power of occupational control, though it may not wash so powerfully through social work or nursing as say through medicine or law, nevertheless provides sufficient opportunities to brighten the prospects of some which previously had looked a little dull. In ditching the dirty work, people-oriented occupations clearly achieve social buoyancy. Yet in so doing, they also expose the myth of a service ideal and reveal some of the qualities needed in the political progress of an occupation.

EVALUATIONS OF THE DISTRIBUTION OF SOCIAL WORKERS AND THEIR CLIENTS

Explanations given for the distribution of client groups amongst fieldworkers often act as a prelude to comments which are either for or against the observed state of affairs. These evaluative remarks concern two aspects of the phenomenon: (i) the presence of bias and specialisation in caseloads, and (ii) the distribution of types of social workers amongst client groups.

(i) <u>The presence of bias and specialisation in caseloads: the specialist-generic debate.</u> Arguments about whether or not social workers should be specialists or 'general purpose' workers (Younghusband 1959) have been a regular topic of debate before and since the formation of SSDs (Stevenson 1981). Although it has been repeatedly pointed out that client groups defined by age and physical condition is not the only basis on which to recognise either specialisms or the concept of 'generic' practice (methods, setting or aspects of service would also do), conventional client groupings remain the prevailing yardstick to describe practice (Booth et al. 1980, p.81; Stevenson 1981). The more theoretical alternatives tend to reverse the traditional model of the client's condition being the basis of the taxonomy and instead take what the social worker does to the client as the basis on which to recognise the specialism. Slowly, but inexorably, it seems that since reorganisation there has been a gradual shift towards recognising and valuing at least some specialisation in practice (Booth et al. 1980, p.v).

(ii) The distribution of types of social workers amongst client groups. There are those who believe that the differences between types of social worker should be recognised and be used as a basis for the differential deployment of fieldworkers. The Birch Report (1976) wanted discrimination in the way staff were used by 'distinguishing those jobs for which social work training, and training in other aspects of social services work are needed and those for which other, more limited forms of training may be appropriate' (McCreadie 1977, p.47).

A different argument regrets the fact that there appears to be so much discriminatory use of staff, particularly as it affects work with the elderly and to some extent the disabled and mentally handicapped. These groups, it is argued, do not receive sufficient attention and understanding from qualified social workers, 'casework skills' and practices that include an appreciation of the psychological and inter-personal (Crosbie 1983; Goldberg 1970; Greengross 1980, pp.34-45; Rowlings 1981; Stevenson and Parsloe 1978, p.144). More rarely recommended is the reallocation of child care work to non-qualified staff. However, Goldberg and Warburton (1979) point out that most of the work with children in long-term care 'is undertaken by qualified social workers ... although a considerable proportion of these situations were very stable and possibly well within the capacity of a mature welfare assistant' (p.103). The prestige that is all too often accorded child care work is to be 'deplored', asserts Stevenson (1978).

CONCLUSIONS

Emerging out of the research studies into social work practice in SSDs are certain patterns and shapes in the way fieldworkers and client groups are distributed with respect to each other. When attempts are made to explain the distribution of work and workers they tend to be couched in terms of the characteristics of the various client groups and how departmental policies view them. No regular underlying logic connects the range of phenomena observed and reported.

Evaluative research in social work, that is research in which 'the goal ... of an activity is made specific, and the purpose of the research is stated to be to examine how the activity has achieved these goals' (Crousaz 1981, p.34), in the main has been confined to the effectiveness of different styles, methods and theories of social work in practice. However, assumptions are often built into these studies about the nature of social work practice. 'Progress cannot be made if we simply <u>assume</u> at the outset the unitary nature of social work as a profession and of the theory that informs it, and then imagine that our deductions from the assumptions produce information about social work activity' (Timms and Timms 1977, p.26). But all too often social work practices are measured against social work's assumed nature. So long as understandings remain presumed or parochial, there will be difficulties not just in explaining the patterns in occupational behaviour but in recognising that these patterns are themselves capable of revealing dimensions of social work beyond whether or not methods are effective or practice bureaucratically restricted.

There is a need to take observations concerning practitioners and their activities outside the domestic arena of social work theory and practice in order to loosen the close knit reasoning that confines our understanding of social workers and what they do. One route in the search for a more encompassing framework of explanation takes us out into the wider field of occupations, their behaviour and organisation. Hence the interest in the distribution of social workers. The research literature offers part answers to the questions 'Surely everyone isn't doing everything?', 'And if everyone isn't doing everything, then who is working with whom?'. However, in order to complete the answers and fill out some of the details, I embarked on further empirical enquiries into the organisation of fieldworkers and their practice.

4 Who is doing what with whom?

INTRODUCTION

The surveys reviewed in Chapter 2 record that different types of fieldworker are more likely to be working with particular kinds of client group. According to the literature, this state of affairs can be explained in two ways. First, the various client groups generate different problems which require different activities and skills on the part of fieldworkers. Second, different types of fieldworkers carry the skills and abilities to conduct these activities in different measures.

It might be expected, therefore, that professionally trained workers holding more sophisticated skills will be found working with cases which are more complex as in work with children and their families. Conversely, the more straightforward work associated with the old is adequately met by the more basic and less elaborate skills of unqualified social workers and social work assistants.

However, rumbling in the background are notes which have an unsettling effect on such tidy accounts of how labour is divided in the area teams of SSDs. There are those who berate skilled and qualified workers for neglecting the old and handicapped (e.g. Brearley 1975; Rowlings 1981). These client groups need and would benefit from the attentions of qualified workers every bit as much as cases involving children and their families. The limited range of practice associated with the elderly and handicapped reflects the limited skills and outlook of the untrained workers who tend to handle work in this area. It does not reflect the limited needs of such client groups.

In order to make some headway into these issues, information was sought about the activities of fieldworkers at the broadest level. The surveys reported in Chapter 2 recognised the heterogeneous and stratified nature of area team manpower. But they begged the question 'what do different types of fieldworkers do?' This suggested a survey which might build on some of the insights provided by the analysis of the earlier data. If work and workers are differentially distributed, what do different types of fieldworker do with different kinds of client group? What activities do different client groups provoke? In short, who is doing what with whom?

A survey of area team social workers was conducted between March 1982 and October 1982. Six area teams from three local authority Social Services Departments took part. The survey was designed to provide answers to the question 'Which types of social workers are doing what kind of things with which client groups?' Information was obtained about the range of activities performed by certain types of social worker with reference to each case held over a four week period. Use was made of the highly versatile 'case review form' devised by Goldberg and Fruin (1976) which was adapted to suit the purposes of this enquiry. Case review forms were completed by social workers for each case which they held. Most of the information on the form related to the type and quantity of activities carried out by the social worker over the four week period immediately prior to completing the form.

RESULTS

The introductory meetings with each area established that 72 fieldworkers were willing to complete forms. In the event 61 social workers and social work assistants took part giving a response rate of 85%. Four social workers were either ill or on holiday at the time of the study. Three more changed their minds about participating. Three social workers never returned the forms; no explanation was given. Forms were completed for 1,267 cases. Table 4:1 describes the distribution of cases amongst the main client groupings.

Table 4:1
Number of cases and client groupings

	number of cases	% of all cases
Old people and the disabled	517	41
Mentally handicapped	106	8
Mentally ill	50	4
Child care and family work	594	47
Total	1,267	100

The distribution of cases reflects the general pattern of work found by other studies which have examined the work of area teams (see Chapter 2). Work with old people and children and their families accounted for 88% of the cases. Relatively few cases (4%) involving work with the mentally ill were described.

THE DISTRIBUTION OF ACTIVITIES ASSOCIATED WITH TYPES OF FIELDWORKER AND CLIENT GROUPS

Information was collected from fieldworkers about the problems they perceived and responses they offered in each of their cases over a four week period. The information was not designed to give a detailed account of the perceptions and behaviours of fieldworkers in each case. Rather it was meant to provide an indication of the type and volume of activity committed by fieldworkers across a range of client groups in a specified period of time.

Information was collected under a number of headings:
1. Problems present (as perceived by the fieldworker)
2. Activities carried out by the fieldworker
3. Agencies contacted
4. Number of home visits by the worker and office visits by the client
5. Number of phone calls made by the fieldworker in connection with the case.

Each area gave a general indication of what was going on in each case. The intensity, frequency and variety of work generated by each case and its fieldworker was derived from the review forms. Fieldworkers were also asked to write a one or two line summary of the aims held for each case during the four week period. Aggregating the results of individual cases allows averages for each activity to be computed for the different types of fieldworker and client group. Tables 4:2, 4:3 and 4:4 describe the averages for the number of problems perceived and activities performed for:

   Qualified and unqualified fieldworkers (Table 4:2)
   Level 1, 2 and 3 social workers (Table 4:3)
   Main client groups (Table 4:4)

The tests for statistical significance have to be carried out on each 'column' separately using the actual numbers and not the average numbers calculated for each case. The calculations require both the actual number and expected number to be determined (see Conway 1967, p.47). If the distribution was found to be significant the letter S occurs beneath the column. If the distribution is not significant, the letters NS occur beneath the column.

Qualified and unqualified fieldworkers

Table 4:2
Summary of work generated by different types of fieldworker

Type of fieldworker	Average number of problems perceived and actions performed per case per month				
	Problems	Activities	Agencies contacted	Visits	Phone calls
Qualified social workers	3.2	3.5	1.2	2.9	3.5
Unqualified social workers	2.6	3.0	1.2	3.2	3.0
Social work assistants	2.6	2.8	0.8	2.0	2.1
p =	<0.001	<0.001	<0.001	<0.001	<0.001
	S	S	S	S	S

On average, it appears that qualified social workers perceived more problems per case, carried out more activities and made more phone calls and agency contacts than unqualified workers who in turn were 'doing more' per case than social work assistants.

Level of social worker

Table 4:3
Summary of work generated by different levels of social worker

Level of fieldworker	Average number of problems perceived and actions performed per case per month				
	Problems	Activities	Agencies contacted	Visits	Phone calls
Social worker Level 1	3.0	3.1	1.3	3.0	3.2
Social worker Level 2	3.4	3.4	1.3	3.3	4.1
Social worker Level 3	3.3	3.5	1.0	3.2	3.3
p =	<0.05	<0.02	<0.001	<0.2	<0.001
	S	S	S	NS	S

Although there are differences between the levels of worker, particularly Level 1 and the others, the distinctions between Level 2 and Level 3 are less clear. Level 2 workers (89% of whom were qualified) appeared to be a little 'more active' than Level 3 workers (all of whom were qualified), but with the only significant differences occurring between the average number of agencies contacted and phone calls made.

Main client groups

Table 4:4
Summary of work generated by different client groups

Average number of problems perceived and actions performed per case per month

Type of client group	Problems	Activities	Agencies contacted	Visits	Phone calls
Children and their families	3.2	3.6	1.3	3.2	3.7
Mentally ill	4.1	4.7	1.7	4.5	4.8
Mentally handicapped	2.8	3.2	1.2	2.9	3.3
Old and physically handicapped	2.6	2.8	0.9	2.1	2.1
p =	<0.001	<0.001	<0.001	<0.001	<0.001
	S	S	S	S	S

In general, child care and family work and work with the mentally ill generated more 'action' per case than work with the mentally handicapped, old and disabled.

THE ACTIVITIES OF FIELDWORKERS HOLDING CLIENT GROUP CONSTANT

The previous section suggests that qualified social workers (who are mainly at Levels 2 and 3) were 'seeing more' and 'doing more' in each case than either unqualified social workers or social work assistants. It is also suggested that work with the mentally ill and children and their families generated more action per case than work with the mentally handicapped, disabled and elderly. As qualified social workers were much more likely to be working with the mentally ill and children while social work assistants and unqualified social workers were much more likely to be working with the mentally handicapped and old people, it may not be so surprising to note that there were differences in the number of activities occurring per case between different types of worker.

If each client group is held constant, the difference in the number of actions per case per month between different grades and types of worker is greatly softened. For example, social work assistants displayed more actions per case when working in the field of child care at a frequency comparable with qualified social workers. Conversely, qualified social workers committed fewer actions per case per month when working with old people compared to work involving the mentally ill. To illustrate this point, work with old people and children is analysed with respect to qualified social workers, unqualified social workers, social work assistants and the level of social worker (see Table 4:5).

Analysing fieldworker types whilst holding constant the client groups of the mentally ill and mentally handicapped is not reported. The number of cases in these categories is relatively small. More critical however, is the distribution of cases within these categories. For example, no Level 2 worker in this survey had cases involving the mentally handicapped, while only two mentally ill cases were in the hands of Level 1 workers. Only one case involving a mentally ill person was being handled by an unqualified social worker. Therefore elaborating the analysis whilst holding these client groups constant became of limited statistical value.

When the client group is held constant the average number of problems perceived and activities performed per case per month by different types of fieldworker became <u>significantly</u> similar. The differences remain between the client groups with child care cases generating more 'activity' for all fieldworkers than work involving the old and disabled. The only exception was in the average number of activities per month for work with old people and the disabled: qualified social workers carried out a higher number of activities per month (3.2 per case) than either unqualified social workers (2.5 per case) or social work assistants (2.7 per case) (cf Goldberg et al. 1970).

Analysis holding the two main client groups constant can be refined further. Examination of (i) the types of problem perceived and (ii) the kinds of activity performed by different fieldworkers operating within the same client group reveals something of the quality of practice as well as just the quantity.

Table 4:5
Summary of work generated by fieldworkers
holding constant the client group

Average number of problems perceived and actions performed per case per month

Client group	Fieldworker	Problems	Activities	Agencies contacted	Visits	Phone calls
Old people and disabled	Qualified social workers	2.8	3.2	0.9	2.2	2.4
	Unqualified social workers	2.4	2.5	0.9	2.4	2.1
	Social work assistants	2.5	2.7	0.8	2.0	2.1
	p =	>0.05 NS	<0.01 S	>0.3 NS	>0.05 NS	>0.05 NS
	Social worker Level 1	2.4	2.5	0.8	2.2	2.2
	Social worker Level 2	2.8	2.7	1.0	2.3	2.1
	Social worker Level 3	2.6	2.8	0.9	2.4	2.4
	p =	>0.2 NS	>0.5 NS	>0.3 NS	>0.5 NS	>0.3 NS
Children and their families	Qualified social workers	3.3	3.6	1.3	3.0	3.7
	Unqualified social workers	3.3	3.9	1.3	3.8	4.1
	Social work assistants	3.2	3.9	1.1	3.1	3.6
	p =	>0.95 NS	>0.5 NS	>0.7 NS	>0.05 NS	>0.5 NS
	Social worker Level 1	3.2	3.8	1.2	3.1	3.4
	Social worker Level 2	3.4	3.9	1.3	3.6	3.7
	Social worker Level 3	3.3	3.7	1.2	3.3	3.7
	p =	>0.5 NS	>0.7 NS	>0.5 NS	>0.05 NS	>0.2 NS

Table 4:6

The frequency of problems perceived according to (i) the type of fieldworker and (ii) client group

Percentage of cases with problem perceived as present

Type of fieldworker	Number of cases	Self-care	Home-care	Loneliness/social isolation	Emotional distress	Family relation-ships	Child behaviour	Child deprivation/abuse	Education	Employment	Financial	Housing	Other
Qualified social worker	773	24	22	28	33	63	41	21	22	11	33	20	5
Unqualified social worker	210	46	42	31	31	51	15	1	12	4	14	14	2
Social work assistant	284	63	48	38	25	32	6	3	3	1	23	16	4
	1,267	S	S	S	NS	S	S	S	S	S	S	NS	NS
Social worker Level 1	262	35	31	30	22	55	24	5	13	7	19	17	2
Social worker Level 2	307	21	27	27	42	64	40	20	29	8	30	21	6
Social worker Level 3	414	30	23	29	31	62	40	22	17	13	33	18	4
	983	S	NS	NS	S	NS	S	S	S	S	S	NS	S
Client group													
Old people and disabled	517	64	50	49	29	30	0	0	1	1	16	17	4
Mentally handicapped	106	47	38	19	30	56	19	2	15	6	23	21	3
Mentally ill	50	64	48	48	64	44	16	12	8	12	44	12	8
Children and their families	594	9	13	16	28	74	57	28	30	13	36	19	4
	1,267	S	S	S	S	S	S	S	S	S	S	NS	NS

S = Significant at the 5% level or below
NS = Not significant

PROBLEM FREQUENCY, TYPE OF FIELDWORKER AND CLIENT GROUP

Table 4:6 reports the percentage of cases in which a particular problem is perceived to be present under the various categories of worker type and client group. For all but 7 out of the 24 problem categories, there were significant differences in the frequencies of problems perceived by different kinds of worker. The balance or 'profile' of problems perceived has a different and characteristic shape for each type of worker. For example, qualified social workers were seeing problems in family relationships in 63% of their cases compared to social work assistants seeing only 32% of the same problem in their cases. However, social work assistants were seeing self-care as a problem in 63% of their cases whereas the same problem was only perceived to be present in 24% of cases held by qualified workers.

For all but 2 of the 12 problem categories, there were significant differences in the frequencies of problems perceived for each client group. The balance or 'profile' of problems perceived has a different and characteristic shape for each client group. For example, problems in family relationships occurred in 74% of child care cases but in only 30% of cases involving the old and disabled. Loneliness was a problem perceived in 49% and 48% of cases concerning the old and disabled and the mentally ill respectively, though the same problem was seen in 19% and 16% of cases involving the mentally handicapped and children respectively.

It can be observed that the statistical profiles of (i) qualified social workers, Level 2 and 3 workers, children and their families and the mentally ill are similar, and (ii) social work assistants and the old and disabled are similar. The profiles of Level 1 and unqualified social workers have characteristics that compare with the profiles of both the mentally handicapped and the old and disabled.

THE FREQUENCY OF PROBLEM PERCEPTION ACCORDING TO THE TYPE OF
FIELDWORKER HOLDING CLIENT GROUP CONSTANT

Tables 4:7 and 4:8 report the percentage of cases in which a
particular problem was perceived by different types of fieldworker within the same client group.

When the client group is held constant, in 43 out of the 48
associations between type of worker and the frequency of
problem perception, no significant difference (at the 5% level
and below) occurred. (It must be noted, however, that the very
large number of child care cases (538) in the hands of
qualified workers compared to the relatively small numbers
being handled by unqualified social workers (28) and social
work assistants (28) swamped the statistical calculations.
This meant that it was less likely for numerical variations in
the categories of unqualified social worker and social work
assistant to assume statistical significance.) The statistical
'profile' is similar between different types of worker handling
the same client group, though the differences between the
'profiles' of each client group is maintained.

Thus, within the same client group the type and range of
problems perceived is broadly similar between different types
of fieldworker. For example, all workers recognised self-
care as the most common problem in work with old people. All
workers perceived family relationships as the most regular
difficulty when working with children and their families.

However there were five instances where there were
statistically significant differences between fieldworkers
carrying cases within the same client group. For example,
child abuse problems were perceived by qualified and Level 3
and 2 workers more regularly than other workers. Given the
policy of most SSDs to allocate NAI work to qualified social
workers this may not be so surprising, although the fact that
some unqualified workers did perceive child abuse problems in
over 10% of their child care cases might not have been
expected.

Table 4:7

The frequency of problem perception according to the type of worker holding client group constant

1. Holding cases involving the old and disabled constant

Percentage of cases with problem perceived as present

Type of fieldworker	Number of cases	Self-care	Home-care	Loneliness/social isolation	Emotional distress	Family relation-ships	Child behaviour	Child deprivation/abuse	Education	Employment	Financial	Housing	Others
Qualified social worker	175	61	54	60	30	32	0	0	0	0	17	21	4
Unqualified social worker	119	64	40	52	34	28	0	0	1	1	12	8	0
Social work assistant	223	67	55	43	22	27	0	0	0	0	13	17	6
	517	NS	NS	NS	NS	NS	NS	NS	NS	NS	NS	S	NS
Social worker Level 1	110	64	40	50	35	27	0	0	1	1	13	10	1
Social worker Level 2	82	60	55	58	31	30	0	0	0	0	16	19	3
Social worker Level 3	102	62	53	61	28	35	0	0	0	0	18	22	4
	294	NS	NS	NS	NS	NS	NS	NS	NS	NS	NS	NS	NS

S = Significant at the 5% level or below
NS = Not significant

Table 4:8
The frequency of problem perception according to the type of worker holding client group constant

2. Holding cases involving children and their families constant

Percentage of cases with problem perceived as present

Type of fieldworker	Number of cases	Self-care	Home-care	Loneliness/social isolation	Emotional distress	Family relation-ships	Child behaviour	Child deprivation/abuse	Education	Employment	Financial	Housing	Others
Qualified social worker	538	9	11	16	29	75	57	29	30	14	37	20	5
Unqualified social worker	28	14	12	14	12	85	85	10	40	14	14	14	0
Social work assistant	28	14	14	7	39	71	71	11	21	0	42	21	0
	594	NS	NS	NS	NS	NS	NS	S	NS	NS	NS	NS	NS
Social worker Level 1	86	15	12	13	18	78	68	12	33	15	17	17	0
Social worker Level 2	213	10	13	15	30	79	70	25	34	12	35	18	1
Social worker Level 3	267	9	10	17	41	74	62	30	29	14	34	19	4
	566	NS	NS	NS	S	NS	NS	S	NS	NS	S	NS	NS

S = Significant at the 5% level or below
NS = Not significant

THE DISTRIBUTION OF ACTIVITIES, TYPE OF FIELDWORKER AND CLIENT GROUP

Table 4:9 reports the percentage of cases in which a particular activity was carried out under the various categories of worker type and client group. 14 out of the 20 activity categories revealed significant differences in the frequencies of activities performed by different kinds of worker. The balance or 'profile' of activities performed is characteristic for each type of worker. For example, whereas qualified social workers performed supervision as an activity in 39% of their cases, this figure dropped to 28% and 9% for unqualified workers and social work assistants respectively. Level 3 workers carried out skill developing activities in 22% of their cases, while Level 1 workers conducted similar activities in only 9% of their cases. However there was no significant difference between the various types of worker in the frequency with which they performed the following activities: mobilising resources (for qualified and unqualified workers), giving information (for all levels of worker), advocacy and group work (for all levels and types of worker).

For all but one of the 10 categories, there were significant differences in the frequency of activity for each client group. The balance or 'profile' of activities performed is characteristic for each client group. For example, the most frequently reported activity for work with the old and disabled (59%) was support and sustainment. For work with children and their families giving information and advice was the most frequent activity (55% of cases). It can be observed that the shape or profiles of (i) qualified social workers, Level 2 and 3 workers, children and their families and the mentally ill are similar, and (ii) social work assistants, Level 1 workers and the old and disabled are similar.

Table 4:9

The frequency of activities performed according to (i) the type of fieldworker and (ii) client group

Percentage of cases with activity performed present

Type of fieldworker	Number of cases	Investigating/ assessing	Giving information/ advice	Mobilising resources	Acting as an advocate	Educating/ developing skills	Helping to solve personal problems	Supervising/ reviewing	Supporting/ sustaining	Facilitating problem solving/ decision making	Providing group activity
Qualified social worker	773	43	52	46	28	19	39	38	51	27	8
Unqualified social worker	210	57	44	52	25	13	25	28	34	13	10
Social work assistant	284	40	62	44	22	4	38	9	54	13	5
	1,267	S	S	NS	NS	S	S	S	S	S	NS
Social worker Level 1	262	58	49	48	24	9	24	12	55	12	6
Social worker Level 2	307	43	51	34	28	18	37	32	40	18	10
Social worker Level 3	414	42	50	46	28	22	40	36	48	26	7
	983	S	NS	S	NS	S	S	S	S	S	NS
Client Group											
Old people and disabled	517	50	56	58	23	6	34	11	59	13	4
Mentally handicapped	106	45	54	41	37	18	24	33	49	12	12
Mentally ill	50	60	68	34	39	28	55	40	58	50	0
Children and their families	594	39	55	34	29	22	38	43	44	29	10
	1,267	S	NS	S	S	S	S	S	S	S	S

S = Significant at the 5% level or below
NS = Not significant

THE FREQUENCY OF ACTIVITIES PERFORMED ACCORDING TO THE TYPE OF FIELDWORKER, HOLDING CLIENT GROUP CONSTANT

Tables 4:10 and 4:11 report the percentage of cases in which particular activities are performed by different types of fieldworker within the same client category. When the client group is held constant, in 35 out of the 40 associations between type of worker and the frequency of activity performed, no significant difference (at the 5% level and below) occurred between the various types of fieldworker. The statistical profiles are similar between different types of worker handling the same client group, though the differences between the profiles of each client group are maintained.

Thus, within the same client group the type and range of activities performed was broadly similar between different types of fieldworker. For example, all types of worker gave information and advice most frequently in child care cases.

However, there were five instances where there were statistically significant differences between fieldworkers carrying cases within the same client group. For example, social workers more frequently undertook investigatory and assessment work with old and disabled cases than social work assistants. It can be noted, however, that no social work assistants in this survey were intake workers which perhaps helps explain the depressed occurrence of assessment in their work. Support work with the old and disabled remained a strong activity for social work assistants (51% of their cases) compared to qualified social workers (22% of their cases) and unqualified social workers (25% of their cases). Supervision and control work with children and their families occurred in 48% of the cases held by qualified social workers but only 17% of those held by social work assistants. This suggests that cases requiring the statutory oversight of children were allocated to social workers and less commonly to social work assistants.

But, although there were some differences between workers which may support the argument that different workers practise differently, there remains the impression that there was an homogenisation of the type and pattern of response made by fieldworkers who worked within the same client group. All workers adopted the broad shape of the client group's 'activity profile'.

Table 4:10

The frequency of activities performed according to the type of worker holding client group constant

1. Holding cases involving the old and disabled constant

Percentage of cases with activity performed present

Type of fieldworker	Number of cases	Investigating/ assessing	Giving information/ advice	Mobilising resources	Acting as an advocate	Educating/ developing skills	Helping to solve personal problems	Supervising/ reviewing	Supporting/ sustaining	Facilitating problem solving/ decision making	Providing group activity
Qualified social worker	175	63	51	76	25	7	35	11	22	14	6
Unqualified social worker	119	54	43	56	18	3	25	13	25	16	0
Social work assistant	223	39	61	45	20	3	33	7	51	8	3
	517	S	NS	S	NS	NS	NS	NS	S	NS	S
Social worker Level 1	110	51	48	52	19	3	28	10	32	11	0
Social worker Level 2	82	58	53	55	27	7	34	11	21	16	3
Social worker Level 3	102	60	50	71	25	9	37	12	23	13	5
	294	NS	NS	NS	NS	NS	NS	NS	NS	NS	NS

S = Significant at the 5% level or below
NS = Not significant

Table 4:11

The frequency of activities performed according to the type of worker holding client group constant

2. Holding cases involving children and their families constant

Percentage of cases with activity performed present

Type of fieldworker	Number of cases	Investigating/ assessing	Giving information/ advice	Mobilising resources	Acting as an advocate	Educating/ developing skills	Helping to solve personal problems	Supervising/ reviewing	Supporting/ sustaining	Facilitating problem solving/ decision making	Providing group activity
Qualified social worker	538	44	53	35	29	23	38	48	56	28	9
Unqualified social worker	28	50	58	22	22	38	29	43	43	17	12
Social work assistant	28	50	62	40	40	16	50	17	49	30	0
	594	NS	NS	NS	NS	NS	NS	S	NS	NS	NS
Social worker Level 1	86	49	59	21	20	30	27	40	40	19	6
Social worker Level 2	213	52	59	34	29	28	38	46	57	31	8
Social worker Level 3	267	40	51	36	30	25	38	48	55	27	10
	566	NS	NS	NS	NS	NS	NS	NS	NS	NS	NS

S = Significant at the 5% level or below
NS = Not significant

FIELDWORKERS AND THEIR CASE GOALS

Fieldworkers briefly recorded their main aim with each case during the four week period. Their aims were categorised according to a very simple scheme, the main purpose of which was to draw out the broad distinctions between the variety of intentions stated by fieldworkers. This gave seven general types of aim. The examples are taken from the respondents' returns.

1. To investigate and assess, e.g. 'I need to visit a couple more times to weigh up what's going on in this family before I can decide what's best to do.'

2. To change the physical and/or material circumstances of the client, e.g. 'To get Mrs R into Part III a.s.a.p.', and 'The DHSS need to realise that Sheila's not getting her full benefits.'

3. To change the behaviour and/or attitudes of the client and/or relevant others, e.g. 'To work with the whole family, hoping to get husband to understand and change his disruptive effect on everyone.'

4. To liaise between clients, other agencies and professionals, e.g. 'At the moment it's important to just keep everyone in the picture so I am acting as a go between mother, Robert (handicapped son), the Home and hospital.'

5. To support and maintain, e.g. 'Low key visits basically to keep in touch and encourage her with the baby.'

6. To monitor the client and the situation, e.g. 'To check on how Linda is feeling towards the baby and its safety.'

7. To control the client, e.g. 'Michael needs to be reminded of how close he is to being removed from home unless he behaves himself.'

The distribution of aims for each type of fieldworker and client group is described in Table 4:12. There were significant differences in the aims set for different types of fieldworker and for different kinds of client group. Aiming to support the client was the most frequently mentioned goal for all types of worker. The monitoring and control of clients was practised slightly more by qualified social workers (19% and 9% respectively) than by either unqualified workers or social work assistants. 29% of cases involving the old and disabled saw workers aiming to change the physical or material circumstances of their clients compared to 10% only of child

Table 4:12
The distribution of aims amongst different types of fieldworker and client group

Type of fieldworker	Number of cases	To investigate and assess	To change physical circumstances	To change behaviour/ attitudes	To liaise	To support and maintain	To monitor	To control	
		Aims (Row %)							
Qualified social worker	773	17	17	12	3	23	19	9	100%
Unqualified social worker	210	10	17	19	2	45	7	1	101%
Social work assistant	284	6	26	5	1	52	5	3	98%
	1,267	df = 12		x^2 = 192.3		p = <0.001			
Social worker Level 1	262	15	17	18	3	36	11	1	101%
Social worker Level 2	307	18	12	13	1	25	18	12	99%
Social worker Level 3	414	14	20	12	3	24	19	8	100%
	983	df = 12		x^2 = 127.3		p = <0.001			
Client group									
Old and disabled	517	11	29	7	4	42	6	2	101%
Mentally handicapped	106	6	15	8	8	56	8	0	101%
Mentally ill	50	12	8	20	0	24	32	4	100%
Children and their families	594	16	10	15	3	24	20	11	99%
	1,267	df = 18		x^2 = 235.4		p = <0.001			

Table 4:13
The distribution of aims amongst different types of fieldworker holding constant cases involving the old and disabled

Type of fieldworker	Number of cases	Aims (Row%)							
		To investigate and assess	To change physical circumstances	To change behaviour/ attitudes	To liaise	To support and maintain	To monitor	To control	
Qualified social worker	175	12	26	6	4	47	4	1	100%
Unqualified social worker	119	10	32	7	1	47	3	0	100%
Social work assistant	223	5	31	4	1	53	4	1	99%
	517								

$df = 12 \qquad x^2 = 16.7 \qquad p = >0.1$

Social worker Level 1	110	12	28	8	3	44	3	1	99%
Social worker Level 2	82	12	24	6	3	48	6	2	101%
Social worker Level 3	102	11	31	6	3	42	6	1	100%
	294								

$df = 12 \qquad x^2 = 3.95 \qquad p = >0.95$

Table 4:14
The distribution of aims amongst different types of fieldworker holding constant cases involving children and their families

Type of fieldworker	Number of cases	Aims (Row %)							
		To investigate and assess	To change physical circumstances	To change behaviour/attitudes	To liaise	To support and maintain	To monitor	To control	
Qualified social worker	538	17	11	17	2	20	22	12	101%
Unqualified social worker	28	14	14	18	4	32	18	0	100%
Social work assistant	28	14	14	11	4	36	18	4	101%
	594								

df = 12 x^2 = 11.64   p = >0.3

Social worker Level 1	86	17	12	14	3	30	18	2	96%
Social worker Level 2	213	16	8	15	4	22	24	13	102%
Social worker Level 3	267	17	12	16	2	20	25	10	102%
	566								

df = 12 x^2 = 18.05   p. = >0.1

care and family cases. Similarly the elderly and mentally handicapped were twice as likely to have support as the goal set by their social worker. Work with children, their families and the mentally ill provoked aims which might be seen as more direct and intrusive. Behaviour change, monitoring and control are cited as the aims in 76% of cases involving the mentally ill and 46% of child care and family work. These percentages fell to 16% and 15% for the mentally handicapped and elderly respectively when the same aims were considered.

Tables 4:13 and 4:14 describe the same range of aims for different types of fieldworker whilst holding constant the two major client groups of the old and disabled and children and their families. As with the problem and activity profiles, these tables show that workers adopt a similar pattern and range of aims within the same client group. There is no significant difference in the aims set between different types of worker involved with the same client group. The pattern and proportion of aims for workers reflected the pattern and proportion of the 'host' client group. Thus, to support and to change the physical circumstances of the client were the two most common aims stated by all fieldworkers, accounting for at least 70% of intentions for most types of worker in work with the old and disabled. In work with children and their families there was a more even distribution of aims although most workers gave support as their first and monitoring behaviour as their second most common intention.

CONCLUSIONS

In terms of problems perceived, activities committed and aims made in each case, the following observations emerge from the analysis:

1. The average number of problems perceived, activities committed and aims made per case differs between types of fieldworker.

    On average, qualified social workers perceive more problems and carry out a greater number of actions per case, each with a characteristic 'profile', than either unqualified social workers or social work assistants.

2. The average number of problems perceived, activities committed and aims made differs between client groups.

    On average, work with children and their families and the mentally ill are perceived to present more problems and generate a greater range of actions per case, each with a characteristic 'profile', than either work with the mentally handicapped or the old and disabled.

3. If the client group is held constant, the average number of problems perceived, activities committed and aims made by different types of fieldworker is significantly similar.

There are indications throughout the analysis that social work practitioners do not entirely control the content and outlook of their own practice. Rather, the client group (the 'work') controls the range and types of activity offered by fieldworkers, determining their perceptions, responses and outlook.

Whereas the survey into the distribution of fieldworkers (Chapter 2) suggested that some social workers are able to control the kind of work they undertake and thus satisfy one important test of professional credibility, this survey reveals potential weaknesses in the attempt by social workers to establish professional control over the content of practice. On first appearance, the survey into the distribution of fieldworkers and their activities suggests that:

> The worker does not control the work; rather, the work controls the worker.

The aims and content of practice appear to be more under the influence of the characteristics of each client group than the social worker's own professional determination. However, this conclusion ignores the organisational and agency context of both clients and workers. The next step in the research was to explore and appreciate the fieldworker and her practice within the broader setting of the organisation.

5 Controlling the content of practice

INTRODUCTION

In order to investigate the nature of an occupation's work and its organisation it is necessary to ask questions about the distribution of workers and questions about the content of practice, particularly as it varies with the type of worker and the different situations met. Thus, 'who is doing what with whom?' became the shorthand question which guided the broad design of the overall research enquiry.

At the end of the third chapter, which posed the simpler question 'who is working with whom?', the results were interpreted to suggest that high level fieldworkers were able to control the types of client group with which they worked: 'the worker controls the work'. The ability of some workers to control the client groups with which they work was taken as an indication that social workers were a differentiated occupational group; higher level workers were manoeuvring to establish a clearer professional identity.

However, this initial picture was revised after the results of the survey reported in Chapter 4 were examined. When the broad content of practice (the activities of fieldworkers) was added to the picture, it appeared that although what was being done varied <u>between</u> client groups, <u>within</u> any one client group the type of worker did not appear to affect greatly the kind of work being carried out. This **suggested** that the characteristics of the client group determine the practices of the worker: 'the work controls the worker'. If one of the basic abilities of a professional is to impose her own logic and understanding on the work, the social worker appears to fall well short of the professional's ability to control the content of her own practice. This at least accords with the alleged 'semi-professional' status given to social workers by many observers (Etzioni 1969).

But one more dimension needs to be added before a final interpretation is offered. The characteristics of the 'raw materials' - the people and the situations addressed by social workers - do not exist as some external, independent given, at least as far as the organisation and its workers are concerned. What the work 'means', how it is perceived and understood and what responses are said to be appropriate in the light of these understandings depends on who is able to control how the work - the raw material - is defined. It is not, therefore, simply a matter of 'the work controlling the worker' as suggested at the end of Chapter 4, but rather a question of how the work is defined and how this definition affects what the organisation's workers do. Taking a step back, it becomes possible to ask who controls what the work means for the organisation (cf Smith and Ames 1976, p.53).

The preliminary results of the surveys suggested that a more detailed enquiry, asking fieldworkers what they were doing and why they were doing it, would help explain the nature of the social workers' practice and the characteristics of their organisation. To this end, information was sought about what fieldworkers saw themselves doing in particular cases and the reasons which they gave for acting in the way they did. Answers were required to a new and different set of questions. What kind of activities, responses and decisions do field-workers describe in their work with different client groups? How do they account for their actions? What are they trying to do and why? What freedoms and limitations do they experience in seeing what they saw and doing what they did? In a nutshell, what did they do and why?

Exploring the locus of control over the content of practice provides information which helps us to consider the way the work is being understood, the way it is being handled and the occupational implications this has for fieldworkers. Using the worker's own descriptions of her practice and experience it is possible to attempt an answer to the question 'who defined the client and the pattern of the worker's responses?'

62 social workers and social work assistants from five

different local authority SSDs were interviewed between March
and August 1982. A broadly open-ended interview schedule was
followed based on a few key questions designed to explore the
occurrence of significant events, decisions and responses made
in specific cases over the previous six months, although background information was also requested. The interviews were
audio tape-recorded and subjected to a content analysis.

RESULTS

The interviews offered examples of different types of fieldworker working with a variety of client groups. The analysis
of the interviews required the imposition of a framework of
some kind in which events and the responses of the fieldworkers
could be viewed. Initially, the fieldworkers' descriptions of
their work were classified along two main dimensions: (i) what
was done and (ii) the reasons why it was done. In both dimensions, the worker also described and explained her work in
terms of the freedoms and constraints experienced in practice.
It was hoped that an appreciation of the workers' responses and
what was felt to determine them would help illuminate who or
what was controlling the content of practice, particularly at
the time of decision making. The descriptions and accounts
were categorised and then related to the type of worker and the
client group. It was necessary to generate a simple framework
in which to arrange the categories. This framework formed the
basis of the analysis which attempted to do two things:
identify the content of practice in terms of responses made and
identify the determinants of that content.

The results are given in four main sections:
1. Types of fieldworker response
2. The occurrence and distribution of responses amongst
   client groups and fieldworkers
3. The evolution of responses within cases
4. Case examples illustrating the types and occurrence
   of control over the content of practice.

1. TYPES OF FIELDWORKER RESPONSE

According to Weeks (1980, p.191), organisational decisions and
responses can be viewed as either (i) routine and programmed
or (ii) non-routine and non-programmed. This simple division
can be used to identify the kind of responses being made by
fieldworkers in the cases which they describe. Prescribed or
programmed responses are determined by people other than the
worker and therefore lie outside her control. Non-programmed
responses remain the worker's responsibility and therefore lie

within her control. Recognition of what type of responses are taking place at important junctures in cases reveals whether control over the content of practice lies with the fieldworker or with other people, such as managers or employers. The locus of control over the content of practice has important implications for understanding the organisation of both workers and their practice.

Programmed responses occur in roles which tend to be routine with low levels of discretion available to the worker. They tend to occur when the work is understood or defined, at least as far as the organisation is concerned, as relatively straightforward. Regular answers are available to familiar problems. All that is required of the worker is to recognise the situation and its characteristics and respond in one of the prescribed ways.

For example, a social work assistant visiting a 79 year old lady living with her daughter described her understanding of the case in this way:

> Well, in cases like this, you know, where the son or daughter want a break, it's usually a simple matter of arranging short-term care in one of our old people's homes. Quite straightforward generally ... uhmm ... fill in a few of the forms we have, that sort of thing and get them organised ...

Here, the worker recognises the case as an example of a problem for which there is an established solution. Senior managers and possibly personal social services committee members identify a need for giving 'carers' a break. Accepting that it is a reasonable need for their SSD to meet, they then determine the kind of resources that appear best suited to meet the need - in this case the provision of a certain number of short-term beds in the city's homes for old people. The social work assistant goes on to describe what she then has to do to secure the resource:

> I have to check that Mrs Albrow is actually fit enough ... er ... you know, not too far gone for an old people's home, so they're not actually ill or incontinent too badly or anything too difficult for them to handle. There's a list of things I have to check and if it's all OK then we can begin to make arrangements.

The worker's actions with the family, particularly the decision whether or not the resource can be offered, lies outside her direct control. The way the case is received, approached, identified, perceived and assessed by the worker is the product of higher management designs. Many of the practical services provided by SSDs have been sanctioned by politicians in the form of legislation which in turn is interpreted by higher managers so that the legislation can be put into some practical operation. The provision itself, the path to be taken to reach it and the determination of an eligible clientele are built into the very way the work is processed. The worker follows the organisation's programme in cases of this kind.

<u>Non-programmed responses</u> are performed in roles where discretion is required in order to cope most effectively with complex, irregular or unfamiliar problems. There are no programmed responses routinely available. The worker has to make 'on-the-job' judgements and use her own occupational skills and experience in the face of exceptional situations.

For example, a qualified social worker, called out to deal with a violent couple with two young children, a case already known to the worker, described the early part of her home visit in this way:

> They were still rowing when I got there; kids crying, that sort of thing ... the usual picture! Tammy looked bewildered. I knew I had to play it just right with these two. I've learned that much with them. If I get it wrong it might end up with Jean (mother) storming out and we may be left with the kids or Alan (father) would go off to the boozer, come back drunk and then I really would have to worry about Jean and the kids. My style with them is to take it quietly, gently, not getting at them at all, you know and just ... just acknowledge ... accept that they were both feeling fraught and angry and helping them both gradually first of all speak to me and through me to the other. Calm down a bit, take the steam out of things and then we could take it more slowly and try to untangle things ...

The worker responds to the particular elements of the case as they exist at the moment. The immediate resolution requires her to judge the situation and decide what range of behaviours on her part would bring about a reduction in the over-heated feelings. These skills are drawn from her own experience and training in such matters.

Perrow (1965) recognises three types of technology available to tackle work. These vary according to whether the <u>materials</u> being handled are uniform and stable or varied and unstable, whether the <u>techniques</u> employed are standardised or exceptional, and whether the <u>knowledge</u> available is able to render the materials manageable or not. 'All three elements of technology combine to influence the nature of individual jobs or "tasks" within organisations', allowing jobs to be described in terms of either 'routines' or 'discretionary content' of work (Perrow 1965). Use of the dichotomy of programmed and non-programmed responses offers a simple basis on which to analyse the fieldworker interviews. To recognise the occurrence, frequency and nature of such responses is useful because it allows an important distinction to be made between:

> areas in which the worker is in personal control of the content of her own practice (non-programmed responses)

and

> areas in which the worker is not in personal control of the content of her own practice (programmed responses).

Recognising who controls the content of practice, particularly in key decision making areas, has an important bearing on a number of matters including the organisation of social workers (issues of 'professionalism'), the nature of personal social services fieldwork and the organisation of fieldwork practice. The characteristics of each of these elements as they occur in SSDs can be picked up in the way fieldworkers describe and understand their work.

'Each social work act', writes Whittington (1977, p.75), 'occurs in the context of some kind of <u>definition of the client</u>. Moreover, the act involves some <u>objective</u> in which the client is implicated'. Whittington (1977 and 1983) sought to classify the 'orientations' held by social workers towards their work. He used an 'action-perspective' which saw workers as 'choice-makers and intentional beings rather than as role players', workers as people who 'take part in creating their social organisation' (1977, p.74). This contrasts with the perspective adopted in the present analysis which recognises the personal views of social workers concerning their practice but sets them within a wider context. In this context the worker's own account might also be 'explained' and her actions and understandings seen as determined by the organisation and the climate of interests in which they are enacted. Whittington (1977) produced an 8-fold typology of social worker 'orientations' covering issues similar to those being raised in this chapter. But his analysis does not pursue the occupational implications surrounding the question of who determines the orientation adopted by the worker. Nor does it raise the question of who has influenced the choice of definitions and objectives with sufficient clarity to enable the typology to be used to detect issues of occupational control. Nevertheless, Whittington's observations have a relevance to the analysis and some of his comments form useful additions to the subject matter of this section.

The worker will find herself pursuing objectives which at any one time might be inclined towards and support the client, the worker and her skills or the organisation. Categorising the fieldworkers' outlooks and actions reveals something of the respective influence of the client, the worker and the organisation on the responses made in each situation. Changes in viewpoint represent shifts in the power to define how matters are to be understood. The various responses record the ability of clients, workers and managers to impose their definition on the situation that faces the fieldworker. Thus, appreciating the occurrence of programmed and non-programmed responses in fieldwork practice indicates with whom and under what circumstances control lies over the work. In effect, the results are a record of the balance of power between the worker and her agency in key areas of practice.

Although the simple dichotomy will be maintained as the basis of analysis, refinements in each category will be introduced. All the examples given to illustrate the analysis are taken from the tape-recorded interviews. People's names and places have been fictionalised.

Non-programmed responses

Because of either the nature of the materials addressed or the end product required by the organisation or the esoteric nature of the skills deployed by the worker or a combination of all three, certain jobs cannot be prescribed in advance. The worker is required to make 'on-the-spot' judgements, responding in the light of what she sees, knows and can do in the situation met. Other than allow the worker control over the content of her own practice in particular acknowledged respects, the organisation's managers have no other way of effecting appropriate changes in the materials, people and situations being handled. In order to be effective, the worker needs 'to ask the reason why of things' (Peters 1966, p.34). The work is therefore said to be under 'professional' control.

Within Whittington's various 'orientations' the workers exhibit particular types of response which can be seen as instances of non-programmed behaviour. For example, within the 'orthodox-expert orientation' the worker directs her attentions towards the needs of the client as interpreted by the worker. The client 'is conceived as possessing a problem and lacking the worker's expert knowledge to define and effect the help or treatment needed' (Whittington 1977, p.79). Changes in the client's behaviour or circumstances are attempted using the expert knowledge and techniques available to the worker. The expertise is described as orthodox because the worker is not questioning the policies and provisions that surround the client and his problem. It is the client who is expected to adjust to the situation.

The following example is given by a qualified social worker involved with a single mother and her four boys on a long term basis. The father left home two years ago. The mother had her first baby when she was 16 years old. At 18 she had boy twins. The previous social worker had expressed concern that the youngest of the four children might be at risk of non-accidental injury. He is now three years old. The social worker said:

> I am trying to help Susan sort out her feelings and help her decide about things like whether or not the twins should go to residential ESN school ... I think that by allowing her to talk and reflect with me this will help her with the kids. Basically my concern is with the children but to talk about, say, her sex life and her boy friend has a bearing on the children obviously, I think, doesn't it, because if she's bugged about something she'll be even more short-tempered with the kids. I suppose what I'm doing is helping her to function better generally so that she can be a better mother I suppose.

Similarly, Whittington's (1977) 'radical-expert orientation' places control in the hands of the worker. The client's problems lie in the prevailing policies and structures and the effect they have on his life. Expert action is concerned with change and adjustment in the policies, provisions, procedures and structures that affect the lives of clients on a small or large scale. For example, an experienced but unqualified social worker, discussing a 76 year old woman in need of residential care, said:

> Ellen moved from her home village of Norton to live with her daughter a few months ago. The daughter lives in our area. Norton is about ... oh ... about 20 miles away I suppose. Well as I said the daughter died unexpectedly and really there was no alternative but for Ellen to go into care. Well our department's policy is for old people to go into homes in the area. But of course Ellen was new and a stranger to our area so I said it would be better for her to go to Norton - there's a home there where she knows people. God, could I get them to be flexible in their bloody rules?! You'd think I was asking to move her to the other side of the world. Well, eventually, after pushing and arguing the case with my Area Officer and then we took it up with the Assistant Director, commonsense at last prevailed and they said she could go to Norton.

The worker, practising non-programmed responses, experiences a freedom of action. The worker has some ability to control the 'raw material' (people and their situations) of practice. There are two types of freedom recognisable in the situations described by fieldworkers: freedom _from_ and freedom _to_. There were situations in which the worker felt there were no limits placed on her practice; she felt free from constraint. And when the worker felt that there was freedom to act, three types of situation were identified: those in which the worker was free to understand and define the work, those in which the worker was free to deploy and practise her 'professional' skills, and those in which new or innovatory steps were taken in order to deal with the problem or need as perceived by the worker. Thus, altogether, four types of situation were recognised in which the worker experienced a sense of freedom.

(i) There were situations in which the worker felt under no apparent restriction. Services were requested and services were given. Advice was sought and advice was offered. Sufficient resources of the appropriate kind, including the time and skills of the worker, existed to meet the needs of the situation as seen by the worker. The following example was given by a qualified social worker working with a 64 year old woman who had had a stroke. The worker felt free to adopt the agency's existing resources but within her own view of what the situation needed:

> I discussed with the husband and his wife, that's Mrs Briggs, what help would be best when she was back at home. We decided that some home help would be useful but not meals on wheels as Mr Briggs felt he could manage. The aids of course the OT was going to see to but they both agreed to talk things over with me when they were together again at home. I thought some counselling of this kind, particularly at this stage would be a good idea.

The next example was provided by a qualified social worker talking with a 76 year old widow who was said by her GP to be experiencing loneliness and difficulty managing at home:

> I generally fix up some day care in cases like this, and some home help, maybe meals on wheels, that sort of thing. There's usually no problem getting them. As I was saying, Mrs Kelly was burgled at about the time of the referral so getting her out of the house as much as possible seemed a good idea.

Most of the examples recording freedom from constraint came from those working with either old people or the handicapped.

(ii) When the worker is free to understand situations as she chooses, she is controlling the way the work is defined. Here, a qualified worker talks about her work with a 5 year old boy:

> I saw this as a case of faulty ... er ... incorrect reinforcement. Danny gets all the wrong cues. Mum ignores him most of the time. She's glad to have some peace and quiet such as when he's just sitting watching the tele or say messing about in the garden, but if he misbehaves or cries, she's there ... either shouting at him or comforting him or showering sweets all over him. No wonder he's getting worse. That's how I saw it. Now I decided that if she could see that switching her behaviour, doing the opposite to what she was doing, I thought we might get somewhere with Danny's behaviour.

(iii) More typically, the worker combines a definition of the situation with the freedom to deploy her own skills and interests. The situation is perceived as an opportunity to practise skills the worker feels she possesses. There are situations in which these skills are practised without any demand or expectation from the client, the organisation or statute. Social workers in these circumstances appear to move into sympathetic 'spaces' within these cases, developing and expanding them in order that their particular or preferred skills might be exercised. The following example is given by a recently qualified social worker dealing with a woman in her late seventies whose self-care and home-care were the subject of critical concern by her GP and brother, and whose only daughter was murdered two years previously.

> Although the case has got many sides to it, I like the emotional things because that's my interest. The practical things in this case are the head-banging ones really but even if they weren't I would still find the emotional things more satisfying; that is where the real issues are and I've started to spend some time in these areas ... I just enjoy poking around people's emotional thingies. I think that's where my skills lie. On a CQSW course the bulk of the work is about the more counselling side of things.

And another example, this time from a qualified social worker involved with a family:

> I've recently done a lot of work with the mother about the death of her first child ... I don't have to be involved at all, though I've chosen to do some work with her. Perhaps I'll close it after we've done the grief work.

Working with a 77 year old man, a qualified worker commented:

> I feel he harbours a lot of guilt about his wife (who died over a year ago) and that is something that we've recently started talking about ... I also wonder if he's come to terms with his horrific war experiences.

The next example is also given by a qualified social worker. His work was with a mother and her 11 year old boy, Neil, who was 'felt to be a bit out of control while his mother was still stuck on the death of her husband three years ago':

> Well it was just after his court appearance that I just happened to get into this very interesting conversation with his 17 year old sister about things that had happened in the past - how obsessive her mum was, even before dad died. I felt this told a lot about the mother and the way she affected family life. It provided me with the material to try some more effective sessions with Neil and his mum; you know, examine with her the way her behaviour affected things, particularly Neil's behaviour.'

The eagerness with which area team workers view work with a therapeutic potential is seen in the next example. Discussing a recently allocated case involving a remarried father to a woman with two teenage daughters, a qualified social worker noted that the father's own daughter, aged 14, was feeling the outsider and was becoming very badly behaved. The worker was enthusiastic about the case:

> It's really classic. She's an obvious scapegoat. It's really good. I think I can do some really interesting work with it ... family therapy is what I'll do, possibly joint work, male and female therapists. I wish we had more cases like this. It really makes you feel you've something to offer.

However, this need to tackle therapeutically promising work is not always recognised outside the area teams. A hospital social worker dealing with a terminally ill patient with cancer due to return home to a distinctly eccentric wife recalled:

> Really it's up to me what I do and how long I keep it. In an area team outside the hospital it wouldn't get visited; it would be a low priority. I can support him ... and his wife and talk about his illness and his death. I think over the years I've developed skills in this area and it would be silly not to use them.

Although examples of the worker's desire and ability to employ therapeutically based skills occurred in all client groups, they received their greatest opportunity in work with children and their families.

(iv) Only one example of practice that might be described as innovatory was met during the interviews. Here the social worker felt free to manufacture a new procedure and resource in order to meet the needs of the situation as she saw them. She described her work with an old wheelchair-bound lady who lived with and 'controlled' her 62 year old daughter whom others felt could do with a break from her over-demanding mother:

> When it's considered that an old person can't continue in the community, we don't seem to have the same sort of considerations as we do for children, and it seems to me that it's just as important for the old person to have the same kind of review meeting before any decision is made at all to place them in an old people's home. It's not departmental policy or in fact practice that we should do such things, but in this case I called a meeting, in their house, of the geriatric health visitor, the GP, the psychogeriatrician, the mother herself, of course, daughter and adopted granddaughter and that group reviewed and discussed the problem and the needs of the situation and what the various courses of action might be ... I now do this kind of conference, review whatever, as a matter of good practice now.

Throughout the examples of non-programmed responses, the ability actually to control the behaviour of people and events remained elusive. Having a calculated effect on the 'raw materials' of the job proved difficult. However, the ability to predict outcomes seemed a little easier:

> She (82 year old woman) wouldn't accept a home help or any support services; no advice from me at all and I knew it would only be a matter of time before she got even worse, more frail, unable to cook or do anything really for herself ... of course it soon got so bad that she had to accept help, quite a lot in the end.

> He (41 year old man) didn't listen to me, not that I expected he would. I knew if he carried on drinking the way he did, spending the housekeeping on beer, being a complete liability as far as she was concerned, she would have to leave him. As I said, he didn't listen and the next thing he knew she was in the local women's refuge.

The experience of freedom appears to be a relative matter. All the case descriptions were set within the broad requirements of the agency and fieldworkers accepted this as their working context. For instance, the resources are provided by the department but often allocated at the worker's discretion. The worker adapts to and accepts the agency's role and expectations of her. Within this agency framework, the worker operates in ways that she feels 'free' to do so. So long as the fieldworker carries out the work expected by her employer, she can choose how to do it. So, for example, violent families have to be visited and their behaviour monitored, but the worker is free to meet these requirements using a variety of methods including the offer of family therapy, the provision of emotional support or the use of psychodynamic casework. In work with old people, their physical safety and welfare have to receive attention, though the worker may choose to offer friendly chats once a week or provide grief counselling.

In this sense, the worker's freedom is not so much to define the basic condition of the client, neither is it to design responses and resources in the light of that condition. Rather, the worker's freedom is greatest in matters of style, tone and manner of response without there being much choice about the underlying character of the involvement. This was particularly true of child care and family work. The one instance of procedural innovation, at least for that worker's own practice, occurred in work with the elderly.

There is less of a statutory jungle covering work with the old and handicapped and therefore practice is legally less cluttered. The established pattern of material resources and service provisions become the main limit on the worker's perceptions and practice. Nevertheless, as the resources are a means to achieving an end, there is scope for workers to modify the means and agencies do appear to be tolerant of changes in this area. In contrast, child care work's statutory ends often entail judgements being made about standards of care and behaviour. There is less emphasis on material provision. The means in child care work are less open to change by the worker. Both the ends and the procedural means place a limit on the worker's freedom of outlook and action. It has already been observed that client groups such as the old and the handicapped are not only the least preferred by the most qualified workers but they are also more likely to have unqualified workers. It might be speculated that client groups like the elderly and handicapped which offer the greatest potential for worker control and freedom of action, at least in terms of interpreting the means, are handled by workers least well equipped to recognise, develop and exploit that freedom. The suggestion is that in spite of fieldworkers feeling free in certain areas of action, there are underlying limits, albeit unassertive in character, which are placed on the responses available to workers. This takes us into the area of programmed responses.

Programmed responses

When the ability to define and design the content of work lies outside the fieldworker's control and with other people (such as managers, politicians or other professionals), her responses may be said to be prescribed or programmed. Although the fieldworker may freely choose to see and do things other people's way, to the extent she has relinquished control over defining and designing what is happening and what needs to be done, she has conceded some occupational power to other groups. Occupations which are unable to control basic aspects of their own practice are thereby weakened.

Pfeffer (1981, p.71) discusses worker responses and decision making in organisations. His comments allow a further refinement to be made to the category of programmed types of response. Decisions and responses can be made not only on technological criteria using the worker's own skills and knowledge ('professional' control), but with reference to the organisation and its design. Thus, decisions and responses can be made:

1. implicitly within the organisation's structure and resources ⎫ Formalised
2. with reference to the organisation's rules and procedures ⎬ Management Control

3. with reference to commands and directives issued by higher management authorities ⎬ Centralised Management Control

In the same vein, Dunsire (1978) notes that basic grade workers choose responses from a limited range of known, pre-programmed options whereas higher grade workers may live in a more contingent universe so that when they search for responses 'it is not so much among options as <u>for</u> options' (p.105). A good deal of basic grade work involves following (i) rules which help classify a 'case', and (ii) rules which help determine the responses once the case has been classified (p.119).

These refinements help generate a two fold subdivision in the category of programmed responses:

(i) <u>Formalised</u>, in which the worker's responses are controlled implicitly by adherence to rules, structures and resources.

(ii) <u>Centralised</u>, in which the worker's responses are controlled explicitly and directly by others more senior and closer to the centre of the organisation.

(i) <u>Programmed responses within formalised management control</u>. The rules of the organisation, the procedural obligations, systems of work processing and the availability of resources all require certain prescribed responses of the worker. By determining the formal rules, procedures and resources of the organisation, managers and politicians programme the kinds of responses expected in defined situations.

The most straightforward type of constraint affecting the worker's response was a <u>limitation in the resources available</u>.

These modify and determine decisions made. Resources may be absent, unavailable or unsuitable:

> I was left in a bit of a quandary. The consultant wanted her (77 year old lady with slight confusion) out of the hospital the next day. I contacted our placement section who said there were no short-term places at the moment so I found myself having to explain our situation to the consultant. I was also wondering if her daughter might help out in some way, just as a temporary measure. (Unqualified social worker)

> I don't see the boy as fosterable. Or rather, certainly none of our foster parents could manage him so I suppose I'll be looking for a suitable CHE. (Qualified social worker)

> The step-father wanted him (16 year old mentally handicapped boy) out. It was getting impossible for Alan. But all there is is some sort of hospital based care. Our hostels couldn't cope with him. (Qualified social worker)

It might also be noted that a resource constraint was not the only limitation operating here. Many workers, in a real sense, were constrained by the limits of their own outlook on the problem and were thinking only in terms of what the department could or could not offer.

The <u>resources available</u> colour the worker's view of the case and what it needs. As Smith and Ames (1976, p.53) ask 'To what extent ... does the work of an area team depend upon decisions about the availability and allocation of resources that are made outwith the team ...?' Assessments and answers are seen in terms of existing provisions so that the worker thinks about the work in the way the established departmental resources implicitly suggest. The client is understood through the filter of services already available:

> She's 90, lives alone in a large house and constantly rings up the police and the Samaritans 'to chat' ... generally she's becoming a nuisance ... her son and daughter-in-law live in a caravan in her garden with their two children ... the son pops in to help out a bit but the daughter-in-law has nothing to do with her what with her being so angry about living in the garden ... it's all made worse for her by her husband's weak attitude.

> After visiting the old lady and learning in no uncertain terms that she wouldn't have a home help or meals on wheels, although to be honest I don't think they would

have helped much, I couldn't see anything else much except permanent Part III but she was dead against it. It's just a case of letting things get worse before we can do something about it; I mean her having to go away. (Qualified social worker)

When other people, not in line-management, are eligible to instruct and advise the worker on the best course of action, the worker may be said to occupy an 'ancillary' role (Whittington 1977). The 'task of the social worker', write Smith and Harris (1972, p.42), 'is simply that of making efficient arrangements for meeting a <u>predetermined</u> need'. In this arrangement, the client is the 'necessary subject of prescription by the referral agent, with the worker a "technician" performing actions to predetermined ends' (Whittington 1977, p.84). Often the referral agent is perceived to possess greater expertise than the social worker. For example, in a case involving a 4 year old mentally handicapped girl:

> The psychiatrist thought a play group or something would help Alison and asked me if I would look into it. I made enquiries and discussed the matter with one or two local play group leaders and eventually came up with a small well-run group that I thought would work well. (Qualified social worker)

<u>Departmental procedures</u>, review forms and check lists act as a potent determinant of the worker's perceptions, understandings and responses. Rules, which can be set at the level of national statutes or departmental procedures, form the basis of many actions. The social worker may act according to the rules willingly or unwillingly, but there are many situations in which these formal prescriptions for action have to be obeyed. The worker visits a foster home because the boarding out regulations require it or the circumstances of a disabled person may be logged to decide on their eligibility for a telephone:

> I go to visit Simon roughly every two to three months in his foster home; about the regulation minimum in fact as there is nothing much to worry about. I end up just having a chat with the foster mum and write up the visit. Nothing else is expected in straightforward situations like that. (Qualified social worker)

Case reviews and conferences are authorised to instruct social workers how to proceed. In fact 12 out of the 24 child care and family cases recorded instances of the worker proceeding according to the advice given by a review or conference:

> We've never been able to prove anything; no injuries on

any of the kids ... I've really got to visit at least once a fortnight, that's been decided at the conference. So generally I call in and keep an eye on things and try and sense how Tracey and mother are relating to each other. (Qualified social worker)

The last case conference had decided that if their Dad (of two young girls) came home drunk again and violent, then I would have to take a Place of Safety. Well, towards the end of the month he really got plastered and smashed up the kitchen and the windows. Really he couldn't cope any more I suppose. I didn't feel too comfortable I must admit but I got a Place of Safety and took the girls to Ashfields. (Qualified social worker)

Along the same lines as conferences directing the work, the statutory expectation that some cases should be monitored and the welfare of the children checked leads workers to stay with the work. A variety of strategies was adopted:

Even if there were no practical problems, and God knows there's enough of them, I would still have to visit whether they liked it or not because there are real worries about the physical safety of the kids, particularly the younger ones. (Qualified social worker)

The major resource of mine is a basic relationship-building thing. I've been quite successful I think like I've offered Dad a lift to his darts match last week when I visited. It's a non-threatening style with them because I need to get a foot in the door ... I suppose there's a bit of dishonesty in the relationship but I've got to get in and see the kids and see how they're getting on ... er ... you see, because we are worried. (Qualified social worker)

I sometimes look at this case and get the feeling I'm doing nothing. I'm not. Things are happening and I'm just bobbing along and yet I've got to keep going. John's got all those offences, mum's on her own with the baby ... who's not well! I can't opt out and I don't know what to do while I'm in! (Qualified social worker)

Review forms and check lists are used to guide the worker through a set of required observations. The record of these observations produces an assessment of the case along specified lines:

What we do in this office with a referral like this is take the SS E1 form with us and check how capable the old person is, you know, it's a form that asks you to check things like, do they cook for themselves or can they light the

> fire and get up the stairs, things like that; so that's what I did when I visited Mrs Atlee. (Social work assistant)

Implicit in some formal actions is the wish to do the 'right' things. Whittington refers to this as a 'defensive orientation' (1977, p.90), which 'represents the worker's intention to avoid or forestall ... complaint and public criticism'. Steps are taken by the worker during her work with the case to demonstrate that she behaved responsibly and correctly. Individual and departmental sensitivity to things going wrong means that there is an unwritten and sometimes written agenda to 'play safe' and this informs the worker's practice:

> They (family with a young baby) didn't want me round really. But given all the signs and the edginess of the GP and health visitor, I'd no choice. There was nothing tangible really. No bruises or weight loss or anything like that, you know, that would stand up in court. Anyway I cover myself by keeping details of all visits, keeping the doctor and health visitor informed, write confirming what has been said or offered ... you know, such things as a nursery place or lifts to the clinic none of which she takes up. (Qualified social worker)

It was suggested that the presence of non-programmed responses revealed the worker's ability to control and manage the 'raw materials' of the job - people and their circumstances. When the character of clients and their situations is recognised as not being amenable to planned changes through the deliberate efforts of fieldworkers, two kinds of predetermined response are possible.

First, only certain aspects of the case are seen as pertinent to the organisation's purpose. These tend to be relatively simple and straightforward and do not require the worker to delve into the complexities of the person and his situation. Aspects of the case which are not relevant to the agency's brief are not taken into account. In this way the case can be simplified and become subject to routine procedures. Determining a person's eligibility for a telephone or acceptability as a private foster parent require only certain predefined characteristics to be present or absent. There is no presumption that the worker's task involves changing the person's intrinsic condition. Control over the situation is achieved by responding only to what is deemed relevant to the task in hand. Thus, formalised programmed responses are based on determining eligibility for the provision of available resources and services, or granting recognition that certain services might be offered:

> We were notified that the Browns were fostering a child privately. I visited and spent some time there. Obviously they weren't the sort of people we would positively choose as a department. I mean there were all kinds of odd, little things that were not ideal but given the fact that the child's parents had chosen them and that there were no compelling negatives in the situation I recommended that things were OK on the private basis. (Qualified social worker)

Second, when it is recognised that behaviour and circumstances are not susceptible to the techniques of the worker or the usual departmental processes, and yet such behaviours cannot be ignored, control is achieved by the imposition of legal and statutory procedures. The use of statutory powers, although it does not alter the intrinsic character of the situation, nevertheless inhibits movement or isolates behaviours that are otherwise beyond control. In effect, matters are controlled by the department and its workers 'clamping down' the disturbed situation using statutory instruments. Mentally disordered people are taken to hospital, children are removed from neglectful parents and criminal adolescents are placed in residential homes. Child care work in particular provokes responses of this kind when no other course of action remains. The worker's responses are programmed to occur when situations are not susceptible to the technical manipulations of the worker and remain legally unacceptable:

> There was no choice in the end. He (13 year old boy) carried on breaking into places - four boxes ... boxes not packets, boxes of crisps was his last job! He's hardly ever at school. I had the police on to me almost daily! I took him into care three weeks ago now ... He's due in court tomorrow. (Unqualified social worker)

(ii) <u>Programmed responses within centralised managerial control</u>. When the worker is instructed or directed to act in a particular way by a manager or a politician, her responses are explicitly prescribed and dictated. Whereas with familiar responses the prescription is embedded in the structure and process of the organisation, in centralised control the directive is clearly on the surface, to be seen and experienced as overt control. Responses and decisions are determined by one set of people and carried out by another. In the following extract, the qualified social worker explained that some foster parents wanted him to reprimand a nine year old foster child for having been particularly naughty (as they saw it). The worker refused and preferred to discuss the implications with them:

> Well my refusal didn't go down at all well with Mr and Mrs

Lincoln. They rang the Area Officer saying they didn't feel able to talk to me because I didn't respond in the way they wanted. Although I wanted to handle it myself, my Area Officer insisted that my senior made a visit with me in which he was to explain I wasn't the disciplining person as such, but there to help and advise. His presence was kind of undermining.

In the following example, the qualified worker's course of action was explicitly prescribed:

The girls (sisters aged 16 and 14) were taken to Court by the Education Department for non-attendance at school. Well, my Area Officer and the Chief EWO had worked up the following plan which was for the girls to come into care for a short period of time, then maybe to return them home 'their lesson having been learned'. Well, I got allocated the case but I couldn't go along with that - <u>their</u> plans - without knowing a bit more. I made a home visit and didn't feel at all sure that coming into care was a good idea. But I've been told I must take the cases and must do what's been decided. I'm not at all happy about this.

Occasionally the worker felt that future decisions were being made by others, but this time by people outside the SSD:

She (mother of two children in care) has been back to Court to try and revoke the Care Orders but lost. The last time all went well until at the very end the magistrates asked ... told me actually ... 'We hope that the children however will be reunited with their mother at some future date'. Well, that set me up nicely with Mrs Austen! That's all she needed to keep on at me. (Qualified social worker)

Randolph and Finch (1977) make the observation that the more routine and predictable the work, the less need there is for communications to take place upwards. The way the work is perceived and the responses made are built into the resources and procedures made available. In contrast, when the work is less predictable, more problematic and not amenable to simple definitions, there is a greater tendency for communications to take place upwards and downwards as clarification is sought and directions are given. Fieldworkers describing work with the elderly and handicapped, involving mainly formalised programmed responses, rarely mentioned the direct involvement of managers. But this was not so in 11 out of 24 cases involving work with children and their families. In these 11 cases, managers, at various levels, became involved at some time, giving specific directions about how the worker was to respond.

In some instances the worker was quite happy about the direction and may well have requested the guidance:

> I didn't know whether to remove Julie (8 year old) or not. The foster parents were getting more and more demanding as well as giving messages about whether they were really the best people to meet Julie's needs, all that kind of stuff, none of which of course was doing Julie any good whatsoever and she was getting worse; unpicking her dresses and being difficult at school; that kind of thing. I didn't know whether to try and work with them or make plans to move Julie to a new foster home or what. I needn't tell you I suppose but it's possible to screw things up for a kid if you get them wrong at this stage. In the end I really put the decision in the hands of our Area Officer ... I put him in the picture completely. He advised me to make another visit to the foster parents and really, I suppose, do a proper assessment ... it was eventually decided to give the foster parents a break and I took Julie to our reception centre. (Qualified social worker)

However, not all workers sought or willingly accepted managerial instruction. The qualified social worker in the next example wanted to receive the child into care on a voluntary basis as part of a general plan of work with the family but practice in his area did not allow him to proceed as he would wish:

> In this area all decisions about kids coming into care have to be referred to the Area Officer. He actually decided. He's got very definite views about how ... on what basis children come into care. He generally does not like the uncertainty of voluntary care so usually we can only have them in care if we get either a Place of Safety or a Care Order.

Non-programmed and programmed responses: concluding remarks

Two main types of response have been described: non-programmed and programmed. A number of variations within each category have been identified and illustrated. In terms of assuming an outlook on a case or taking decisions which affect the organisation's resources or legal responsibilities, programmed responses predominated. However, once the fieldworker is working within the agency's definitions and prescriptions, the style and manner of action are likely to remain under the control of the worker. Or, more cynically, the organisation does not mind <u>how</u> the worker conducts her practice so long as she carries out the agency's requirements. These requirements reflect the legislation that informs the various roles that social workers can take in practice. They fall into two main types:

(i) The provision of resources and services to which the public may seek access or the social worker may recommend
(ii) The responsibility and authority to judge standards of behaviour and circumstances and act in the light of these judgements on behalf of the community.

When practice is prescribed or programmed, it is with reference to one or other of these areas of responsibility. And as the statutory resources and obligations of SSDs appeal to different client groups, it might be expected that the various kinds of programme described appeal more to some client groups than others. The distribution of the different types of response picks up these basic statutory distinctions.

2. THE OCCURRENCE AND DISTRIBUTION OF RESPONSES AMONGST CLIENT GROUPS AND FIELDWORKERS

Most cases witnessed a number of types of response being employed by fieldworkers during the course of their involvement. Although the analysis of interviews noted when different responses were occurring, recording the exact number and frequency was not possible. The gradual evolution of responses or the reassertion of the same type of response at various stages of the fieldworker's account made specific numerical comparisons between cases difficult. However, it is possible to comment on whether or not particular responses were commonly adopted or rarely employed by either particular types of fieldworker or all types of fieldworker handling particular client groups within the limits of the small number of cases described.

Only four cases describing work with the mentally ill were available. In each of the cases the worker saw herself adopting responses which were non-programmed in nature. Two out of the four also employed responses that were categorised as formally programmed. The association or clustering of certain types of response in work with particular client groups appeared as a strong theme throughout the analysis. Formally programmed responses were employed regularly in work with all client groups. Centrally controlled responses were most commonly present in cases involving children and their families.

Fieldworkers' descriptions of their work in child care matters regularly identified both non-programmed and programmed responses. All but one case (held by a social work assistant) showed instances of responses of a non-programmed nature. 21 out of 24 of the child care cases contained examples of formally programmed responses. In 11 child care cases, the worker's practice, at some time, was explicitly directed by a higher departmental manager. In four cases, this specific direction was followed unwillingly and became a source of conflict between fieldworker and manager.

All but four of the 34 cases involving the physically handicapped, mentally handicapped and elderly displayed examples of formally programmed responses. The physically handicapped (five out of 10) produced proportionately more responses of a non-programmed kind than the elderly (three out of 17).

3. EVOLUTION OF RESPONSES WITHIN CASES

In many cases the pattern of responses changed with time and also varied depending on the type of client group. Using the two predominant client groups of work with children and their families and work with old people, the types of response were examined chronologically within cases. Although there were shifts within cases, there tended to be a flow in the direction of the type of response with respect to time from non-programmed to programmed in work involving children and their families:

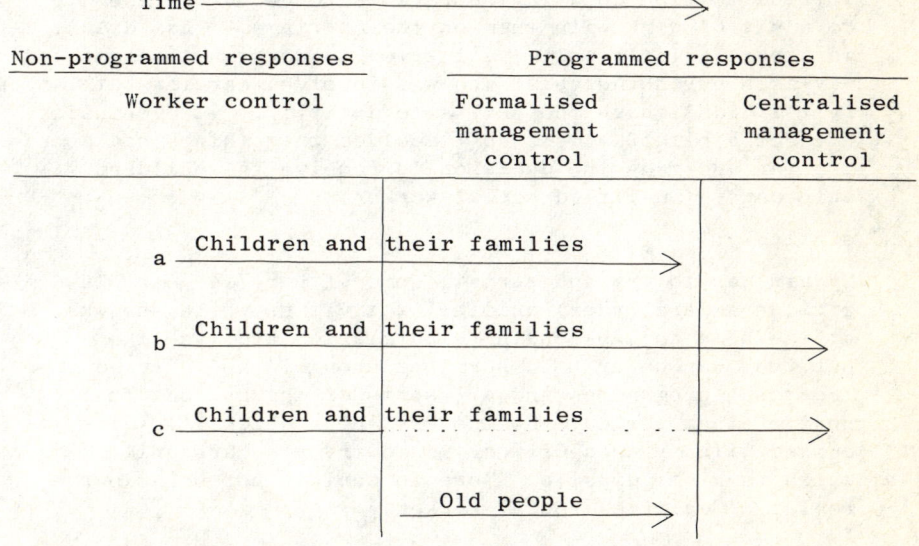

Work with old people remained under the influence of formally programmed responses throughout. Non-programmed responses did take place in some examples, but they were secondary in influence and did not account for the evolution of the case. In child care and family work there were situations in which the worker, believing a course of action to be desirable, then found that she had neither the personal resources nor skills available or that they were insufficient for the job.

The main initial strategy adopted was <u>for the fieldworker to redefine the situation</u>. This was particularly so where the worker had to stay with the case for statutory reasons. Only if the worker's redefinition was viewed as inadequate by a manager was a further evolutionary stage reached in which <u>the manager defined the situation and directed the response</u>.

Redefinitions of the work in this manner saw the type of responses shifting from non-programmed, generally therapeutically inclined responses to the worker accepting departmental procedures as the most suitable course of action. Instead of attempting to cure people, behaviours and situations were 'battened down' by the use of statutory and procedural powers brought to bear on complex and troublesome matters. Although this did not 'solve' the problem, it clarified the position of the various participants and obliged people to declare their positions and the nature of their involvement. The worker accepted that she was acting as an agency functionary and not an independent practitioner:

> I tried to link up with the parents to encourage them to do a bit of work with them on the marriage. That didn't work particularly well ... I tried to work in the same way as a psychotherapist who was involved earlier but I felt I didn't have the skills to do it ... It eventually all got a bit of a mess so I decided that things had gone too far and made the decision to receive the children into care. (Qualified social worker)

And similarly:

> My aim was to try and curtail some of her (14 year old girl on a Care Order) criminal activities while she was at the home and absconding - burglaries and the like - but they can never hold her long enough. We've tried treatment programmes and all sorts of things, but they've none of them worked. So the next plan which I've discussed with my Area Officer is to try a secure unit which is a bit drastic. More to contain her behaviour really. (Qualified social worker)

In the next example, the qualified worker was attempting to work with a school truant whose recently widowed mother was feeling she could no longer cope with him:

> I worked out a plan - a programme with the mother to get Alan (aged 14) back to school again. It didn't work out at all well, even when I arrived at nine in the morning

to help things along. Things got worse and Alan went to
Court for still not going to school. He was already on a
Supervision Order and so we went for a Care Order and got
it. Given our lack of success with Mum and his going to
school, we were obliged to do something about him.

The complexity and volatility of many cases is such that the
worker appears simply to be <u>tossed along by events</u>, with little
professional control over the 'raw materials' being apparent.
The phenomena is very similar to Davies' (1981, p.59) notion of
'turbulent fields'. The worker appears to react to events,
being forced eventually to adopt a formally programmed response:

> It all presented itself as a bit of a mess. The mother
> said she was going to kill her husband if he didn't stop
> drinking, she accused the 15 year old son of being a homo-
> sexual, the girl was said to be glue sniffing ... My
> proposal was to meet and work with the whole family and
> to try and make sense of ... er ... this, well mess, you
> know, to get them talking and understanding what was going
> on ... It never really worked out that way. When I
> visited at the arranged time mother would usually rant
> and rave, father was never to be seen and the kids wander-
> ed in and out. In between visits I'd get frantic phone
> calls from mum and the school would say they were getting
> more and more worried about Tracey. This went on for
> weeks with me trying to keep up with them all until the
> police got in touch. They had Simon and said he'd been
> sexually assaulted. His mother refused to have him home
> ... in the end we had to receive him into care.
> (Qualified social worker)

And again in the following case in which a 71 year old man
and his 40 year old wife had two young children:

> This family has all kinds of problems and regularly erupts
> violently ... literally ... and then denies massively
> until the next crisis ... (later) ... Mother came in
> with the two kids and a bag of clothes saying she couldn't
> cope any more and we could have them ... This is a scene
> we've played through so many times. She leaves them and
> comes back at five o'clock, a bit calmer, collects them
> and goes home, though in the process she is still verbally
> and quite often physically violent. I've no control how
> it works out and it's always extremely wearing ... I
> felt rather traumatised by this whole latest experience
> even though I'd been through the thing so often before.
> I was close to taking a Place of Safety on the kids and
> a Section on her. You see with this kind of violence
> around and the madness in the air there was considerable
> worry about what it was all doing for the kids. The

reviews were clearly saying that if it happened again and
the kids continued to be seen as disturbed then I ought to
be trigger happy for statutory intervention and she must
understand this and what the agency's views were. I then
had to discuss it with my senior to decide whether really
I ought to get hold of the situation. (Qualified social
worker)

In work with suspected child abuse cases, Dingwall, Eekelaar
and Murray (1983) characterise the first period of involvement
as obeying the 'rule of optimism'. A variety of justifications
is used by the worker to minimise the chances of parents being
considered guilty of harming their children. If the parents
show a lack of cooperation or the problem has not been contained by the actions offered to date, the case moves into the
procedural framework of case conferences and if the evidence
is sufficiently worrisome and watertight, care proceedings
ensue. The 'rule of optimism' has parallels throughout child
care work. However it applies only so long as the worker is
perceived as not losing sight of the agency's statutory role.
If the worker fails to recognise the need to move into the
procedural mode her responses are liable to be dictated; they
will be centrally programmed by higher managers:

Certainly the children's behaviour - lots of acting out,
very disturbed behaviour in many ways - their behaviour
was being adversely affected by the parents' repeated and
frightening rows. As I said their mother was Greek; very
fiery woman ... I started marital work with them ... but
they couldn't really understand what I was getting at.
They couldn't understand the connection between what was
going on with the boys and what was going on between them.
Looking at the marriage just seemed to baffle them ...
It was my intention to change tack a little and try some
individual counselling with each of them before trying the
two of them again, but a case conference was held at this
time and the consensus of opinion, from all sides - except
me! - from our Area Officer in the chair and the school,
was to go for care proceedings and then maybe place the
kids in a special school for maladjusted kids. (Qualified
social worker)

The original case conference decided that the original
injury, which was a cigarette burn inflicted by the
parents on Marie (aged 3), though the parents have always
denied it, was non-accidental. The case conference
decided that the case should be given to me on the understanding that if the parents would accept voluntary supervision from me I was to stay involved; I was to try and
gain a relationship, but if it didn't work out then it
would all be reviewed ... I must admit that although it

was slow, I felt I was getting somewhere, at least I was
invited in rather than being kept talking on the doorstep!
Nevertheless, another accident - Marie came in with a cut
and bruised head - her mother said she'd fallen out of the
downstairs window where she'd been messing about - another
accident resulted in her ending up at casualty. I know
mum is careless about supervising Marie but I've never
been convinced it was deliberate. Anyway the paediatrician
was unsure and the conference decided really I had no
choice but to take it to Court. (Qualified social worker)

When cases become immune to both the techniques of the
worker and the procedural responses of the organisation, there
is still a requirement that the worker stay with the case. The
worker 'sticks by' the people involved, even though there is no
immediate hope of improvement. This is what workers do 'when
all else has failed' as one worker put it when describing her
work with a difficult teenage girl in care. When technical
expertise and statutory authority do little to check people and
their behaviour, to stay with the situation is all that remains
to the worker and her organisation, particularly when the case
cannot simply be abandoned:

She's (14 year old girl in care) bloody obnoxious most of
the time. She makes it very difficult for anyone to like
her. At the moment it's all downhill - running away, more
offences, more aggression - it's like she doesn't really
give anything to anybody because they're going to reject
her so she gives up trying ... I think hanging on to her,
not writing her off is important for me. I must not give
her up like everybody else ... there's not much else we
can do! (Qualified social worker)

The feeling of just being tossed along by events and yet
needing to stick by the client is a common combination and is
illustrated in the following example:

We've discussed the children's play, but I wouldn't say
we've got very far with that. I think she thinks I'm
stupid or at least she just smiles at me and lets me
rattle on. She ... uhmm ... treats the kids like mates,
you know, tells them everything about her boy friends and
things and Emma's only 4 ... (and later) ... It would
be nice to think or say that I'd actually made her have
more control over her money or her emotions or her ability
to feel like a parent to the kids but in fact what I seem
to be doing is just be around when the next disaster
occurs - a huge gas bill, one of the kids swallowing dis-
infectant, Julie (the mother) wanting to give up ...
(Qualified social worker)

4. CASE EXAMPLES

The following three case examples are given in greater length. They illustrate in detail how the types of response and the associated kind of control over the content of practice vary with time. The two cases involving work with children and their families illustrate the evolution of responses from non-programmed through those which are formally prescribed to those which are managerially directed. In particular, the responses made when events were judged to be critical will be highlighted. The characteristics of the client and his situation as well as the demands made by others in the worker's environment influence the development of the case and the degree of control experienced by the fieldworker.

Case A

Unqualified but experienced male social worker working with an 81 year old woman, Elsie Gardener. This case illustrates the worker responding in a programmed manner in terms of (i) the department's responsibility for the provision of services for the elderly, and (ii) the department's resources and procedures made available when working with the elderly. The worker views the client 'through' the resources and responsibilities provided.

Background: Elsie lives in an unmodernised terraced house with an outside toilet. She has arthritis. She lives downstairs and has a commode. Forgetful but independent. Her niece (wife of a vicar) calls in several times a week to do her shopping. She has a home help one morning a week for three hours. However her sister contacted SSD to express concern that her elder sister, Elsie, was not looking after herself properly and was deteriorating: 'She should go into an old people's home'. The social worker visits and describes his meeting as follows:

> Her opening words before I managed to say anything except who I was were, 'Oh, will you empty my commode'. Well, fortunately it only contained a dribble of urine so I did it. Then I had a chat about her sister's worry and idea but it was clear that she wouldn't consider Part III. She certainly liked chatting though so I thought of day care for her - company and that - she could natter all day there, but she wouldn't consider it even though I think she is rather lonely and likes contact.
>
> I was going to close it on returning to the office as there was obviously not much to be done but I got a phone call from the next-door neighbour, a young family with children. Complaints that Elsie was emptying the commode down the

outside drain which they shared.

At first I didn't react, but then I got a phone call from another neighbour saying in no uncertain terms 'what was I going to do about it?' I went round next day but could see no evidence of her emptying it down the drain - nothing, no bog roll remains, nothing. I asked Mrs Gardener but she swore blind she would never even consider such a thing. So what I did, really, in a sense, was put the frighteners on her to make sure she didn't do it again ...

She's refusing all the usual supports so I'm thinking of closing it. I'll discuss it with my senior to see what she thinks about staying involved. I've gone through the department's range of options with Elsie. She either doesn't like them or she's not strictly eligible. She doesn't want day care, Part III's out of the question and she's getting as much home help as we can give her and so there's really nothing else we can do.

Case B

Graduate, male qualified social worker. This case illustrates the worker's initial attempts at unprogrammed 'professional' responses. This did not alter the problematic behaviour which remained as the central concern to the department and other professional groups. The worker was encouraged increasingly to adopt prescribed responses which at various times were set within (i) formalised management control systems, the worker following procedural and statutory guidelines, and (ii) centralised management control systems in which the worker's responses were dictated by managers.

Background: Family with material problems; poor housing. Poor standards of child care reported by the health visitor and the housing department. Standards of hygiene described as worrying by the health visitor.

The parents had little knowledge of how to rear, bring up children. Only young. Both were ESN, little idea of what children's needs were. I see our role as trying to support them, trying to keep the children at home because it was other agencies that were continually pressing for something to be done about the children, i.e. for them to be actually removed from the house.

Although I did share some of the health department's concern, I didn't think things were bad enough to remove the children. There were certainly problems - failure to thrive, poor stimulation, delayed milestones, all this sort of thing. But when the two eldest boys reached 4 and 5 they were past the vulnerable stage ...

But with the arrival of another child - she's now about 12 months old - the whole problem started up again - underweight, several illnesses ... The health visitor, the GP, the hospital were all expressing concern. After the birth the baby was in hospital with a bronchial infection. I must admit that when I got involved when the child was about four months old, I wasn't particularly concerned ...

There've been almost continuous case conferences. I was reasonably happy though, knowing the family. I assessed the family really - there's lots of difficulties I know - but they're a family of survivors who always manage just to keep their heads above water and despite the underweight, I felt that things were reasonably good. It was quite strange for me to go to the case conferences and hear everyone criticise them ...

All the kids were on the 'at risk' register. There was no suggestion of ill-treatment. It was failure to thrive.

At the case conferences on the baby were the health visitor, the GP, hospital doctors, my Area Officer and senior and me.

Well, last autumn, three months ago, the normally stable relationship between the parents deteriorated. She got a boyfriend, didn't seem to spend much time at home, didn't express much interest in the kids and that was something that was quite new to the situation ... an added strain and worry really. I found a nursery place for the baby so we could monitor it as well as provide it with stimulation and give it a day time feed as well. So I'd got some real support there, practical as well as everything else. I also met mum and dad and we discussed the worries and their feelings and behaviour and I thought these went quite well.

But she (the baby) didn't always attend the nursery regularly. There were quite long periods when she took the baby to her (mother's) aunt. The baby's weight was still very underweight and this was worrying and the medical opinion was that the baby was very vulnerable ...

However, I still felt that things were reasonably OK. The weight became the major indicator that things were not that good although I honestly felt the baby looked OK. It seemed that when the baby went to the aunt's its weight went up and when it went home it went down or did not improve. Using this as an indicator to say that the child was at risk ... it was decided, under great pressure at a case conference in October that if there was any loss of weight I would have to take some action ... in fact some of them (members of the case conference) wanted the baby to come into care there and then.

However, I did feel that there were a lot of positive features too in the household ... I felt at the time of the case conference that the right decision had been reached that we would wait and see... The medical lobby still kept on about things like hygiene, you know, things like the toilet being filthy, maggots in the wet washing or so they said though I never saw them, but there was certainly a lot of pressure on us ...

What happened next was that only a few weeks after that case conference the child had lost weight! I went along to the Area Officer and said 'you know the child's lost weight' and his immediate reaction was 'take a Place of Safety'. I was saying 'Hold on. Let's look at what the circumstances have been in the last week or so'. The baby had been ill, she's had diarrhoea. I was accused by the Area Officer, actually accused of making excuses to avoid the baby coming into care. I'd decided that a Place of Safety was premature. I couldn't see the evidence standing up in court ... Eventually the Area Officer accepted my decision. The medical people weren't happy about this but I felt I was looking at the case not from just a medical view but also from a social point of view in terms of looking at the family and how their commitment to the child was and their abilities.

A month later there was no obvious improvement - no clear weight gain ... The parents were thinking that the child might go to the aunt's over Christmas because she'd be better looked after which seemed quite responsible in one way. But the parents' attitudes towards the child were changing too - less of a commitment to her particularly requesting the child going at Christmas of all times.

I tried to persuade them against this because I felt that some of the weight loss was due to the fact that she'd spent periods here and there. I'd thought I'd succeeded - I'd even ordered a taxi to take her to the nursery because of the snowy weather - but in fact they'd taken the baby to the aunt's for the Christmas period. I'd also decided to get a home help in - a home educator I suppose really. The baby came home back from the aunt's in the New Year after having had chicken pox there. So eight days had been spent with the aunt and then seven days in the New Year with the parents and when she was next weighed there was a weight loss.

So, yes, I felt yes, there had been a weight loss but what does it mean? What can we do with that fact? Whose fault was it? But I was advised that I must abide by the case conference and go ahead with a Place of Safety Order.

Up till then my work with the parents I suppose was basically policing the situation ... well at least as they saw it. Work with them was quite difficult. A lot of what I did was practical with a little bit of family and casework. I got bedding, visited twice a week, that sort of thing. I did some work with the parents. I did quite a bit with Kenny, the husband, who seemed to be coping better with the situation than his wife and to try and get him to express some of his anxieties he had and the difficulties he had in trying to keep his wife with him because there'd been times when she wanted to go, clear off. I didn't do so much with the wife. Quite a strange woman really to work with and I'm not sure how I could have tackled things with her.

Anyway, I took the Place of Safety Order. My view throughout the case is that whilst very young, yes, there were problems and they would be vulnerable, but once they got out of babyhood, no real worries. So on the day of the Place of Safety I was still not happy with it, I must admit, but I think that what was developing was that we'd been messing about with this case so long, let's take some action was what people were saying ... All the members of the case conference were telling me that there were enough signs now that I couldn't ignore. But I must admit that I was still feeling reasonably happy, I mean ... er ... I felt reasonably confident but my position was now relying on instinct, intuition, no concrete evidence, just feeling.

To be quite honest in this kind of situation I automatically think what are the saving graces, what really has happened, how do we avoid taking drastic action ... I look for positives. So as I felt that as the evidence wasn't clear, I argued with my Area Officer about taking the Place of Safety Order. But in the end I took it. I had to take it.

I felt by this time I'd got no real option. I felt a fair amount of professional compromise. I wasn't totally happy about the decision, but I felt I was against the wall, really. Even though I was still trying to get people to climb down on decisions but ... er ... but the Area Officer, who was also the case conference chairman you know, was taking a hard line decision now. So I took the Place of Safety. It was difficult. The child was placed with foster parents. I explained the situation to the parents. I think also ... that ... er ... because it was an act of omission rather than commission it's more difficult, particularly trying to prove it in Court.

Case C

Graduate qualified social worker; female. This case illustrates some of the limits experienced by the social worker in determining the direction of practice decisions because of (i) the momentum of the case itself which evolved without apparent reference to the worker's professional actions and (ii) the dictates of management via policy (formalisation) and personal directives (centralisation) in the face of worker resistance. However, practitioner freedom of a kind was eventually established but not based on technical skills, rather on moral conviction.

Background: Billy (now 13) was born in Belfast to a single Roman Catholic mother, living with her parents. She'd already had three children. Eventually the youngest two, including Billy, were placed, as babies, in a residential nursery with a view to adoption. But when Billy was 4 his mother became involved with a Protestant man. Her local community disapproved and the man was shot in both knee caps. Billy's mother left Belfast for England with her two eldest children and arrived homeless. They were housed and she married her Protestant boy friend. Billy and his sister Kelly were taken out of the nursery and joined their mother in England. There were constant difficulties and SSDs were always involved. Most of the care given to Billy and Kelly was provided by their slightly elder sister Mary. Both parents began to drink heavily and the mother disappeared for days at a time. Their stepfather asked for Billy, Kelly and Mary to be received into care again when Billy was 7. The eldest child was permanently placed with her stepfather's brother. Two months later the mother returned and had the three youngest children home again out of the children's home. Three months later she disappeared and once more they went into a children's home. Their most regular visitor was their maternal grandfather but after six months of their second episode in care he died. The hope at that time was that all three children could be fostered together. They were all also receiving therapy at the psychotherapeutic clinic. A foster home for three could not be found so the decision was made to foster them separately, or possibly keep Billy and Kelly together.

When Billy was 11 he was placed with a family who had six children of their own plus one adopted child who was a couple of years younger than Billy. It was hoped that Mary might join Billy but the foster parents didn't take to her. Three months after Billy's arrival in the foster home the foster father died. The family's children blamed it on Billy: 'Billy arrives, father dies'. The adopted black child was becoming highly disturbed. Billy's behaviour also became very disturbed. He was fat, destructive and very depressed. The foster mother also became chronically depressed and went for psychiatric treatment. She wanted Billy removed and so he was taken to a temporary foster home. Whilst in short-term care the present social worker became involved and picks up the story:

> The short-term foster home wasn't a very positive experience for Billy. He became more and more difficult; acting out all the time. I was actually quite pleased that he was showing that something was wrong but it was difficult for the foster family to handle even with counselling from me. They were a German family. Although the foster mother was quite caring, the foster father was quite punitive towards Billy. He became quite aggressive to the boy. After four months they said he had to go. Of course we'd been looking like mad for some long-term home but hadn't come up with anything.
>
> I think at this time I had got fairly locked into fostering ... yes, another fostering! That was to do with (the Borough's) official policy as well; they're very pro fostering, and really at that time I wasn't in a position to question it. Looking back we really looked at some quite unsuitable families. I looked at one family who we introduced to Billy and he had about two visits and then they said they didn't want to foster at all so that was another rejection. We looked at an adoption family but they didn't want him after a number of visits.
>
> Then this year we looked at ... I looked at a single male adopter who ... er ... and he was quite unsuitable. I ... uhmm ... I found him quite a difficult person and I wouldn't want him having a child placed with him, not because he was a single male, but because he just didn't seem suitable.
>
> Anyway, in lots of ways, I was beginning to think that Billy wasn't suitable, ready for adoption. It wasn't on. He still had lots of feelings about his own family and I was beginning to feel also that fostering wasn't on because I thought that they - the foster family - would have to be so exceptional and that really that was what I was worried about and I didn't want Billy to get back into his conforming, subdued behaviour which is what would have happened in the family I think and I really wanted to get out the more disturbed side of him which I couldn't imagine a family coping with. I could see that I would need to develop my work with him a lot further before he could cope with a family. So in view of this plan I was beginning to think in terms of specific types of residential care.
>
> Of course, I have to discuss my ideas with my senior.

I cannot make decisions without that. But my senior's OK. Now, as I said, they (the Borough) have a policy about fostering. It must be the first choice always and you have to have very, very good reasons for thinking something else. You have to explain alternatives ultimately up to the Deputy Director of SS, though in most cases the decision to place is sanctioned by your Area Officer.

Because there wasn't an appropriate family for Billy I could see we were actually making things worse for him by this confusion over placements. I was also beginning to think the original decision to go for adoption was quite an off-assessment. He needed to work through what his own family meant to him, his sisters, his mum being in prison and being so violent.

Well, while I was doing all these things the German foster family said they were going on holiday and Billy would have to leave before they went. That meant another short-term holiday place. I then got into a huge row with the Central Group who arrange and determine fostering and adoption because I said I didn't want to use the single male adopter. And they basically interpreted this as me not wanting to use single male adopters which wasn't what I was saying at all. It was about Billy and it was about this particular bloke. Eventually it got quite heavy, to put it mildly. The Deputy Director stepped in and said that I <u>had</u> to place Billy irrespective of what I thought. I had to place him with this bod on a 28 day placement (as a single male he cannot foster except by way of leading up to adoption) ... I was ordered. I was told if I didn't do it then someone else would. The case would be taken away from me. I felt horrendous to put it mildly. I felt at the time that what I was doing was wrong for Billy and I shouldn't, but, well, if it was going to happen I could perhaps protect him a little bit because he knows me and I would actually stick with him rather than let someone else handle it.

The adopter turned out to be very manipulative ... he bought Billy loads of things and I think Billy was tempted but bless his heart he said he hated it. He really didn't like it ...

So Billy stayed there the 28 days in which time I was still battling with the Central Group so we had to place him again because Billy so clearly didn't like it and so Central backed down although they said that I was making the wrong decision. Well, my Area Officer became involved and saw my side and started looking for a therapeutic community home, but before we could come up with anything we had to place him somewhere else and the only thing that they came up with was with the (Borough's) only other single male adopter! Which was unfortunate! Billy went and had a very, very disturbing month, a most damaging period ... anyway there were lots of things going on about these issues that I was never really aware of. Quite hairy really.

Well the deal eventually was this: if Billy went into residential care the first male adopter could visit and take things more slowly. In six months the situation would be reviewed.

So Billy went to the Home and I think he's gone from strength to strength. He's a lot more delinquent in inverted commas - he's really acting out much more. He's quite a changed personality ... when ... much more able to express his worries and anxieties and really he's quite difficult. The Home really has a handful with him. I respect the way the Home works. Billy's got security there and relief. Predictably the male adopter hasn't visited much. The staff thought he had a bad effect on Billy.

A lot of the work we've been doing with him is around really petty type stuff, you know, like petty shop-lifting, smashing car windscreens, absconding to Macclesfield ... you know, really 'naughty' behaviour ... acting out, just being able to express his anger and things. I see him once every week or two and we talk around his family, his mother and he feels potentially very violent and it's to do with having internalised this myth about her rather than the reality. I'm trying to make her a real person ... she's not a monster, she's quite pathetic really.

CONCLUSIONS

Organisationally, the critical areas of practice in field social work are those which have implications for both the department's resources and its statutory raison d'etre. The interviews leave one major impression: that key areas of practice were controlled by managers as they interpreted and operationalised the political and legal remits of the personal social services. Although the manner of practice was open to interpretation by fieldworkers, control over the content of practice lay outside the purview of practitioners and rested with managers. Managerial control was most often exerted implicitly through organisational structures, formal procedures and the design of resources. Overt control, though less commonly experienced, did occur, particularly in child care work, taking the form of managerial commands to individual fieldworkers on how to behave and proceed.

6 The control and organisation of work

INTRODUCTION

Two major observations emerge from the surveys:
- (i) Fieldworkers and their work are differentially distributed
- (ii) Fieldworkers perceive various limits to their practice, experienced either explicitly in the form of direct control by others or implicitly in the way that structures and procedures inform the conduct of work.

Both observations describe key features in the organisation of fieldworkers and the organisation of their practice. The argument will be that the two observations are manifestations of the same basic condition in the character and make-up of social work. By describing the distribution of social workers and the constraints on their practice it is possible to shed light on the nature of the work. In turn, this provides a basis on which to explain both the organisation and standing of social workers as an occupational group.

Definitions of social work by social workers tend to be both generous and ambitious. Even so, there is a feeling that all is not well in the state of social work. Professional recommendations are made on how to improve the stature of the occupation within large welfare organisations. These professional recommendations contain a number of 'understandings' about social work and the origins of its weaknesses.

(i) Social workers need to improve their professional standing by, for example, establishing a stronger body of knowledge or clear code of ethics. This strategy accepts the analytic assumptions of the trait approach to understanding and promoting professional success in which an inventory of key attributes is extracted from their general make-up. Analysing professions in this way has been a particularly attractive method of proceeding for the aspiring professions. In the way clothes are alleged to maketh man, donning the garb and habits of the established professions is thought to do wonders for the appearance and character of those in jobs who are not sure about their social standing but aspire to a more substantial image. There are no more avid observers of the professional scene than those who want to get it right and pass for the real thing. As Katz (1964, p.71) wryly remarks, few professionals talk as much about being professionals as those whose professional stature is in doubt.

A large number of attributes have been coaxed out of the classical professions of law and medicine including such things as a body of knowledge, a code of ethics and control over training. There is no doubt that making lists of professional attributes is straightforward. It is attractive to would-be professionals because it gives them a clear idea of where they are and what they feel they must do in order to improve their occupational lot. It is a cosy exercise too. The established professions feel comfortable, for it confirms their self-image. Semi-professions are encouraged; after all, inventories can be enlarged. But if professional attributes are the symptom and not the cause of an occupation's standing, then social workers have been chasing the shadow and not the substance. The persistent 'semi-professionalism' of social work suggests that there is something about the activity which renders face changes of a cosmetic kind useless.

(ii) Society fails to appreciate the true worth of social workers as they tackle the disadvantaged and the deviant. In order not to feel misunderstood and undervalued, the public needs to be educated about the real merits of social workers (Brogden and Wright 1979). In essence, what is now referred to as the 'functionalist approach' (Johnson 1972, p.31) saw professionals doing work which the rest of society believed to be important and valuable. The approach posits that the professions are service or community oriented occupations applying a systematic body of knowledge to problems which are highly relevant to the central values of the society (Rueschmeyer 1964, p.17).

Most dominant values have a conservative flavour. They are concerned with preserving, restoring and transmitting the customary state of affairs. Health, conduct, labour and money are all encouraged to remain within 'normal' and 'proper' bounds. Any group which offers to preserve, restore or transmit health, personal conduct, money and the like will be of considerable interest to those members of society who have the most to gain from things remaining roughly as they are. The professions 'strike a bargain with society'. For behaving with competence and integrity they can control their own affairs and receive generous rewards. It seems that the professions are good for society, so society is good to the professions.

(iii) Social work practice is constrained by its being housed in bureaucratic organisations which are restrictive. If social workers could be free of bureaucratic management, 'real' social work practice would flourish. This line of argument suggests that, for no clear reason, social workers just happen to find themselves in large bureaucracies, the managers of which perversely impose unreasonable limits on practice (see e.g. Miller 1968; Piliavin 1968)

Although there are grains of truth in each of these 'analyses', essentially each misses the point. It would be more productive to ponder the fact that social work is a relatively weak occupation compared to the 'established' professions and that social workers do tend to be organised in large welfare departments run by managers. It is then appropriate to ask 'what is it about social workers and what they do which regularly finds them organised and arranged in a particular way?'. It may be only natural for social workers to wish that things were otherwise, but for the sociologically inquisitive the current patterns of practice and organisation themselves are the subjects of interest for they represent a statement by society and its dominant interests about what social work means.

In Chapter 3 an attempt was made to explain the differentiation of workers and their work within an interactionist framework making particular use of the concepts of 'clean' and 'dirty' types of work. Within this framework, credit is given to practitioners who work out how to increase their professional standing by attempting to monopolise prestigious areas of practice. The approach hints at the self-interest of occupational groups. However it fails to deal satisfactorily with why some 'professional projects' succeed and others fail. It says nothing at all about why social workers and their practices are organised in the way they are in large welfare bureaucracies.

The task of providing a more comprehensive explanation of social workers and their organisation is helped by turning to recent theoretical developments in the sociology of occupations and organisations. Absent from most home-grown accounts of social work, both as an activity and as an occupation, is a willingness to set explanations within a broader structural context, relating social work to wider organisational and societal interests. Current sociological literature in this field allows observers of social work to take a step back from the profession-centred parochialism that has tended to dominate 'explanations'.

UNCERTAINTY

Not knowing how things are going to behave or situations turn out are sources of potential uncertainty. Living with uncertainty is uncomfortable. Generally people try to avoid it. But if people do have to live with uncertainty, attempts are made to understand, control and predict it so that it no longer generates feelings of discomfort or unease. Most occupations are about imposing order and predictability on materials and situations that otherwise appear haphazard.

Different occupational groups tackle particular aspects of the environment. The environment might be material objects or people. Certain features of the 'work environment' will be of direct concern to those workers who attempt to control and manipulate parts of the environment in order to bring about particular valued ends. Depending on whether the job involves fashioning metal into the shape of a plough, giving people chemicals to stop them feeling ill or talking to adolescents to get them to behave more acceptably, the characteristics of the 'materials' addressed and the techniques used may or may not be able to bring about a predictable state of affairs. Difficulties met in the 'work environment' represent uncertainties in the workers' ability to bring about desired outcomes. All occupational groups seek to reduce uncertainty; that is they attempt to increase control over their environment. Uncertainty might lie in the obduracy, complexity or volatility of the materials or people being considered. It might also lie in the efficacy of the techniques available to handle such objects and people.

However, what is recognised as uncertain depends on the preferred outcome. The fact that iron expands when hot, for example, does not greatly bother those who manufacture bicycle frames but it may be of considerable concern to those who build long bridges in tropical climates. In other words, uncertainty is only pertinent if it impinges directly on the plans, practices and understandings of the worker, although as we shall see, some occupational strategies choose to ignore, circumvent or redefine uncertainty as a way of establishing a type of control. If the skills required to deal with the uncertainty are difficult, complex or not easily acquired and the need to control the object is particularly valued, those who possess such skills are well placed to assert their views and interests in the matter. This ability is likely to increase the power of that occupation.

Crozier's study of organisations which made a very simple commodity, tobacco, illustrates the relationship between uncertainty and occupational power (Crozier 1964). In most of the factories the workers operated within a highly routinised system, most events being regular and predictable. The exception in this otherwise clockwork world was the maintenance men. They were responsible for machine maintenance and repair. Without well-functioning machines, all else ground to a halt. The aim of this group of workers was to keep this key area of work under their control, free from outside interference or rationalisation. Only they knew how to fix the machines which had stopped. By controlling the last major source of uncertainty, the maintenance men gained in power. The introduction of new equipment into the factory which could be handled more simply and routinely, would remove much of the uncertainty which was the source of power for the maintenance men. Such a change would shift the balance of control towards the organisation's directors. In this sense, the problem of uncertainty would be resolved by the directors and more power would flow their way. Dependence on the knowledge and skills of other groups adds to the weakness of an occupation.

If coping with uncertainty allows an occupation to control its own practices, thereby increasing in power, three types of occupation might be recognised:

1. Those which control their own work
2. Those which control their own work and the work of others
3. Those which have their work controlled by other occupations.

In practice many occupations contain practices which relate to more than one category. Nurses, for example, might have areas of their work defined by doctors but they may also seek to develop more independent areas of nursing practice. The preference and pressure on most occupational groups is to increase control over the content of their own practice wherever and whenever possible.

These introductory remarks give shape to two notions that

will be useful in examining social workers and their organisation. The first involves the idea of <u>control</u> over an occupation's practice and the other, more nebulous at this stage, hints at the <u>competition</u> that may take place over who is able to determine the style, content and direction of an occupation's practice. Obviously control and competition are closely related ideas and both can be used to increase our understanding of work and its organisation. The literature in this field is wide-ranging but the themes of control and competition will be used to review the subject of occupations, work and organisations in two broad and related areas:
1. organisations and their management; 2. the professions.

7 Managerial control

CONTROL OVER UNCERTAINTY IN THE PRODUCTION PROCESS

Uncertainty, including the presence of insufficient control over the elements of production has been employed by Marxist writers examining the relationship between capital and the labour process. To the extent that the ability to reduce uncertainty in the production process remains in the hands and minds of workers, the owners of capital and those who manage on their behalf do not have complete control. The capacity to cope with critical aspects of the production process and organisational uncertainty is a source of power. Asserting control over the production process (to secure reliability over profit-making) is generally achieved in two basic ways:

(i) The design of the overall shape, order and components of the production process lies with managers. Individual workers have no clear understanding or creative part to play in the total productive act so that managerial agents decide 'what would be made and how the job would be done' (Hill 1981, p.7). Fragmentation of the work into smaller tasks is often a corollary of management design.

(ii) Coordination of the productive process and a 'sense' of the overall 'shape' of the endeavour lies only in the minds of the managers.

These two methods of gaining control have received considerable attention in the literature and can be considered under the broad headings of <u>de-skilling</u> and <u>coordination</u> of the work process.

DE-SKILLING

Braverman (1974), using a Marxist perspective, attempted to explain the prevailing pattern of productive technology and the associated labour process. His basic assumption is that labour under capitalism is geared to the creation of profit rather than the satisfaction of man's needs, with the consequence that the very nature of work is dominated and shaped by the accumulation of capital. This creates fundamental conflicts of interest between workers and capitalists. The transformation of work under capitalism therefore leads to major problems of control. Braverman argues that Taylor was the first management theorist to recognise the need for a new system of control. In this way class relationships are said to enter the very nature of industrial technology.

> Workers who are controlled only by general orders and discipline are not adequately controlled, because they retain their grip on the actual processes of labour ... To change this situation, control over the labour process must pass into the hands of management ... by the control and dictation of each step of the process, including its performance. (Braverman 1974, p.100)

Taylor's systematic analysis of work leads to its 'decomposition', 'degradation', or 'de-skilling'. The following features emerge out of Taylor's notion of 'scientific management' (Hill 1981; Littler 1982; Salaman 1982):

1. Work is fragmented into its simplest, routine and unskilled constituent elements. Individually these elements mean little to those set to carry them out. Routine work is programmable. Work is therefore divorced from the skill and autonomy of the individual worker who thereby loses control over the content of his own practice. The worker's area of discretion is lost and with it his organisational power. However a few workers in this process are required to develop detailed skills over a limited area ('specialise') and become responsible for matters such as innovation, regulation and repair. All of which means that the process of fragmentation leads to an increase in the division of labour.

2. The shop floor loses the right to design and plan its work. There is a systematic separation between planning and doing, conception and execution, mental and manual, 'brain' and

'hand'. Taylor wished 'to take all the important decisions and planning which vitally affect the work of the shop out of the hands of the workmen, and centralize them in a few men, each of whom is specially trained in the art of making those decisions and seeing that they are carried out' (Taylor quoted in Clegg 1979, p.130). The principles of work design constructed by managers constitute a strategy of control. Therefore 'it is management which "deskills" workers' (Salaman 1982, p.49).

3. The divorce of 'direct' and 'indirect' labour progressively suppresses that part of the worker's activity which consists of preparing and organising the work in his own way.

4. The redistribution of tasks amongst unskilled and semi-skilled labour results in the cheapening of labour. The skills required in fragmented labour are minimised. The time needed to learn a job or task is reduced to a minimum. This being the case, the worker becomes easily substitutable.

The routinisation of tasks in organisations achieves two things (Pfeffer 1981, p.272): it reduces the amount of uncertainty present in the task and makes those performing the job more replaceable. Together these mean that workers have less control over their work and therefore less power. With less power, their decision making ability and the discretion they have in the organisation is weakened.

COORDINATION

Taylorism is said to embody a 'dynamic of deskilling' (Littler 1982, p.52). However the reintegration of the fragmented job-roles requires knowledge and systematic management of the overall production process. As the only group in a position to appreciate the whole process, control also passes into the hands of management through acts of integration and coordination. Workers who retain some control over their work constitute a potential source of uncertainty for managers. Work degradation and standardisation permit prediction and programmed planning (Salaman 1981, p.160). Thus, labour becomes more 'manageable'. When jobs are de-skilled, the market power of workers vis a vis managers is weakened.

ORGANISATIONAL STRUCTURES

The organisation and its design express the arrangements made to control and carry out work (Salaman 1979, pp.102-42). Organisations, therefore, are structures of control. As a form of control and regulation, organisational structure includes the design of the division of labour, the hierarchy of authority and the operating rules and procedures that people follow in their work. The result is that power and control are no longer explicit but 'embedded in the structure of the organisation' (Edwards 1975, pp.9-10). For example, McCleary (1975, p.209), examining probation officers in America, concluded 'that what appears as a free exercise of discretion on the part of the probation officer may actually be a structurally constrained forced behaviour'. As there are different types of organisational structure identifiable, so there are different kinds of control being asserted.

For the early theorists, such as Weber and Marx, organisations were most interesting as mechanisms of control. Weber's model of bureaucracy stimulated an important strand of thought in the analysis of organisational structure and managerial behaviour. It was thought that the most efficient models of bureaucracy contained, amongst other things, pyramidal hierarchies of authority, clear cut divisions of labour and specialisation, and formal bodies of rules and procedures. Based on the concept of rationality, organisations seemed to mean both technical efficiency and control by adherence to rules which were impersonal and therefore impartial. The advantage of bureaucratic forms of organisation included specialisation of competence, precision, reliability and the removal of personal discretion on the part of workers. Control is centralised and extended by 'the establishment of explicit regulations and procedures that govern decisions and operations' (Blau and Shoenherr 1971, p.348). To Weber, bureaucracy therefore meant control by experts - those with the skill and knowledge to be able to apply the technical rules and norms that govern the functioning of organisations.

As the classical model of bureaucracies received various revisions, and exceptions were noted, it was recognised that in fact a variety of organisational forms and managerial structures existed. However, differences occurred in the way organisations were being thought about on each side of the Atlantic with Clegg recognising an American and a European style (Clegg 1979, pp.2-3). Americans tended to adopt a behavioural focus, turning to organisational psychology and looking at 'man-in-organisation' for explanations. Their emphasis was functional. They were interested in what went on <u>inside</u> organisations. Relations with business were essentially cooperative, with a stress on 'people' and 'goals'. In this framework was born the Human Relations school in which harmony within the organisation was valued. In contrast the European emphasis was on structure. Here the concerns were with identity and power. What went on between the organisation and its host society was seen as important. Hence there was a greater use of sociology, particularly conflict-based accounts, in organisational analysis.

The distinction is important. Much of management thinking has been inspired by American organisation theory and, as it will be suggested later, the practices of business management have been a major knowledge base for public service managers, including those in the personal social services. Work designs and managerial techniques in the personal social services owe a great deal to industrial practices. But in order to understand how organisations and the practices of their workers relate to the rest of society, the European tradition proves to be the more trenchant and rewarding.

Salaman (1981, p.187), addressing the prospect of analysing the mechanisms of organisational control and structures, describes three major approaches (within the European tradition):

1. The neo-Weberian approach, which emphasises the relationship between the varieties of organisational form and the nature of the organisation's environment, its size and market.
2. The Durkheimian tradition in which organisational structure and mechanisms of control originate in the organisation's goals and the technology employed.
3. The neo-Marxists, who revive capitalism as their key variable. The pursuit of profit, the conflict with labour and the need to control the production process characterise this approach. Taylorism has already been mentioned in this context, but the extension of this analysis into an examination of power within organisations deepens the understanding.

These approaches to the study of organisations and occupations have produced an extensive body of literature which will be examined briefly under three headings:

(i) Organisational structure and the environment
(ii) Organisational structure and technological determinism
(iii) Organisational structure and power.

(i) Organisational structure and the environment

Organisations operate in a social, political, economic and physical context. This forms its 'environment', aspects of which may be of direct concern to the organisation such as changing market needs, statutory demands, public expectations, and the steadiness of a regular technology. The structure of the organisation might be <u>contingent</u> upon the environment

(Pugh and Hickson 1976), or the 'success' of an organisation might be contingent upon its utilising the most appropriate structure for its environment (Bowey 1976, pp.51-52). The structures and control patterns that 'suit' different environments received early attention in the work of Burns and Stalker (1961). Based on their study of various factories, Burns and Stalker recognised two types of organisational structure:

1. Bureaucratic or 'mechanistic' types which exercised control through centralised, rule-bound procedures and decision-taking. Work is fragmented into prescribed tasks which are enacted in set situations in a regular manner. This form of organisation is most appropriate in environments which are stable and settled. Events and therefore responses are reasonably predictable, routine and unchanging. The 'environment' and organisational responses can therefore be rationalised. Structures tend to be hierarchical and pyramidal.

2. Professionally oriented or 'organic' types in which decisions and work control are delegated to workers on-the-spot whose own occupational know-how and skill are independently brought to bear on the work in hand. The jobs of workers are not 'fixed' and vary in the light of their judgement of what the situation needs. Structures therefore are non-bureaucratic, prescriptive rules are few and decisions and discretion decentralised. This gives organisations which are flatter and less pyramidal in structural shape. This form of organisation is appropriate in unstable environments characterisited by rapid change 'which give rise constantly to fresh problems and unforeseen requirements for action which cannot be broken down or distributed automatically ...' (Burns and Stalker 1961, p.120).

Initially these two types of organisation suggest that control and power reside either centrally with managers or have been decentralised and lie with relatively autonomous workers. However, Blau and Shoenherr (1971) introduce other mechanisms whereby control is centrally retained although decisions can be taken by 'shop floor' workers. They employ the concepts of centralisation and formalisation to explain the ways in which managers may retain control.

Centralisation refers to the place where decisions are taken in the organisation. In highly centralised organisations all significant decisions are made at the top. Delegation is kept to a minimum. Supervision is widespread. However, if decisions have to be taken quickly or where technological innovation, expertise and flexibility are important, centralised decision making may be restrictive and costly.

Formalisation describes how workers can be controlled and 'constrained through their subjection to a large body of defined rules, regulations and procedures' (Salaman 1980, p.81). Control is gained by the worker's adherence to a set of rules which is sufficiently comprehensive and detailed to determine his or her responses. Decisions can only be understood as products of particular organisations and their resources. The real power remains at the centre, but there is less need to refer decisions upwards. In a sense, the decisions have already been taken. They lie with those who constructed the rules and the manner of their interpretation. Large sized organisations prevent top managers making all decisions directly but high formalisation ensures the whole system continues to operate along predetermined lines.

After reviewing the work of a number of authors but particularly Child (1972) and Duncan (1972), Shortell (1977) identifies five dimensions to the organisation's 'task environment': (i) complexity refers to the number of external factors with which an organisation has to contend, (ii) diversity refers to the extent to which the external factors are different from each other as to the nature of the problems that they pose for the organisation, (iii) instability refers to the rapidity with which external factors change over time, (iv) uncertainty (unpredictability) refers to the extent to which (a) the occurrence of external factors can be predicted, and (b) the nature of the problem or content of the event can be predicted, (v) hostility is defined as the extent to which the external factors pose a threat to the organisation's goals and objectives.

According to Shortell, success for organisations depends on their ability to adapt their internal designs to the various dimensions present in their 'task environment'. So, for example, 'organisations operating in environments characterised by a high degree of complexity, diversity, instability, and uncertainty will also have more fractionated goal structures and non-routine technologies ... In contrast, those operating in very simple, low diversity, highly stable and predictable environments will have a more integrated goal structure and routine technology' (Shortell 1977, p.287). Thus, according to 'contingency' theorists, the way organisations perceive (or even 'choose to see', as will be argued later) their task environment will influence the structural design and control patterns of the organisation.

(ii) Organisational structure and technological determinism

Whereas the contingency theorists look to the environment for an understanding of structure, there are others who prefer to consider the organisation's technological base as the way to analyse structure. The 'socio-technical' approach argues 'that given a commitment to a specific organisational goal, organisations develop and install appropriate technologies to get the work done, and that these in turn have a major impact on the structure of the organisation and, most pertinently, for the organisation of control' (Salaman 1981, p.153).

In her research, Woodward (1969, p.196) found that 'when the firms were grouped according to similarity of objectives and techniques of production, and classified in order of the technical complexity of their production systems, each production system was found to be associated with a characteristic pattern of organisation'. Three types of technology and their associated structure are recognised:

1. In unit batch, 'special order' or 'made-to-order' production, control is relatively simple and inclined towards 'organic' types of structure. Work is mostly unprogrammed and craft-like. Design and execution are in the hands of the same workers.

2. In continuous flow production such as oil refining, the machinery, the organisation of the plant and its work contain built-in controls. Workers act as 'trouble-shooters'. Overall decisions about the production process are left to automatic and computer systems. Design and execution are in the hands of separate workers.

3. In mass production systems, the link between technology and type of control is less close leaving management able to exercise some choice, although in general organisations tend to be bureaucratic and 'mechanistic'.

Implied in this classification is the important recognition that the 'technology itself represents, among other things, a form of control, or at least the possibility of control, such that when technology is designed which contains built-in controls and directions, other forms of heirarchical control are not necessary' (Salaman 1981, p.154). Perrow (1972a) looked at organisations and the things that they do (their technology) to raw materials. 'He suggested that the stability of the materials used and the extent to which regular routines could be devised to deal with them determined the ways in which work roles could be defined' (Hill 1981, p.80). The greater the uncertainty or unpredictability of the materials, that is the number of exceptional cases encountered in the work, the less organisational roles can be structured. This leads to increased worker discretion and autonomy.

Hage and Aiken (1969) use Perrow's idea about technology to analyse the 'people processing organisations' of health and welfare institutions. People and their problems were seen as raw materials which are either routine and stable or unique and unpredictable, depending on the organisation and its outlook. A family agency scored high on viewing its clients as routine. Clients were interviewed in a set, predetermined fashion in order to establish whether or not they were eligible for material aid. The organisation at the other extreme was an elite psychiatric family agency in which experienced therapists worked autonomously and approached clients with no preconceived administrative framework. Hage and Aiken conclude that people/processing organisations with routine work were more centralised, formalised (using procedures and policy manuals) and prone to use staff with less professional training than their therapeutic counterparts.

However Perrow introduces another important dimension to the 'raw materials' of the organisation. As well as their inherent stability and variability, the raw materials can be more or less understandable in terms which matter to the organisation and its technology. <u>'He emphasises that these distinctions do not refer to some actual state of the raw material, but to the way in which it is considered and defined within the organisation'</u> (Salaman 1980, pp.67-68, emphasis mine). Organisations attempt to define their raw material to 'minimise exceptional situations' (Perrow 1972, p.51). This opens up the way for procedural routines and rules. Perrow's analysis is important because it suggests that the environment perceived, the raw materials addressed and the technology used are not inert predetermined givens. They can be chosen and defined by people in positions of control and power.

(iii) Organisational structure and power

Marxist theorists regard the design of work in organisations and the choice of technology as devices to maintain control and so reduce some of the uncertainties over the accumulation of profits. Managers are no longer viewed as a passive but an active occupational group very aware of their interests and ways of thought. Decisions about how the division of labour is to operate and which technology is to be used are taken by managers. Organisational structures are not the consequence of any inevitable and inescapable logic of environment or technology. Hill (1981) concludes that 'managerial policy rather than technology is the crucial variable' (p.99). Thus organisational structure is the product of policies as much as economics with successful groups arranging things to suit their interests. The design of work represents the means by which managers implement their ideas about control.

Task environments, raw materials, the technologies used and

the value placed on the workers' skills available are defined
by those in control. It is their understanding of what the
organisation is about and how it should operate which holds
sway. Rules and constraints are built into the very workings
of machines, procedures and the resources available. And lying
behind such rules are those in control and able <u>'to establish
the premises upon which organisational decisions are taken'</u>
(Salaman 1980, p.82, emphasis original). As Gouldner (1976)
sees it, there is an intimate relationship between ideology and
technology, with technology being used to confirm ideological
regimes. Even where worker discretion is present, the freedom
is more apparent than real. If managers cannot control workers
through technological means, then equally potent is the control
of worker decisions through <u>normative</u> or <u>ideological</u> means
(Anthony 1977, p.2; Hill 1981, p.16). Ideologically, workers
accept the prevailing perceptions and understandings of those
in control. Such workers can be trusted to make decisions in
line with the general ideological climate of management (Fox
1974). Whereas direct control through technological means may
be effective when there is no effective worker resistance, as
in Taylorism and work decomposition, ideological means remove
the very ability to think of resistance and recognise clashes
of occupational interest. Workers are committed to the aims
and style of the organisation. Those granted discretion
already identify with the organisation and the goals of management. 'Friedman and Fox', says Salaman (1981, p.172), 'suggest
that the (relatively) high-discretion strategy is most likely
to be applied to those employees performing central, key
functions, whose commitment is most important'.

Many of these issues have been brought together by Clegg
(1979, pp.116-149) in his consideration of power, control and
structure as they occur in organisations. Using Offe's (1976)
distinction between 'task-continuous status organisations' and
'task-discontinuous' organisation, Clegg builds up an argument
about the nature and manifestation of control and power within
organisations.

In 'task-continuous' organisations, all members at all levels
share the same technology and rules. Superordinates differ from
subordinates merely in terms of greater mastery of the rules
and greater ability, knowledge and experience over the matters
in hand. Weber used task-continuous organisation as it occurred in the military as his ideal-type bureaucracy. The product
organisation of the small craft workshop, with master, journey-
man and apprentice is typical. Power clearly derives from
ownership and control, with explicit directives being an
appropriate form of instruction.

But with the growth in the scale of production, artisans

became workers, tasks became fragmented and managers conceived though did not execute the work. This describes the task-discontinuous organisation in which different workers at different levels are doing and understanding different things. That is, 'the mastery of the technical rules of a subordinate position is basically <u>not</u> an essential component of a superordinate position' (Clegg 1979, p.118, emphasis original). However, because of task-discontinuities, there is the prospect that some low level workers may be able to control areas of uncertainty and thus achieve some (usually) modest power (e.g. Crozier 1964). Control therefore becomes a problem as the organisation grows. Personal orders from the owner or commands in military-like task continuous organisations or ideal bureaucracies are no longer effective in task discontinuous organisations. So, concludes Clegg (1979, p.121): 'As organisations have grown in size, and become qualitatively differentiated in terms of their specialist skill composition ... the balance of the basis of power shifts from one side of Gramsci's dual perspective - that of domination by coercion and command - to the other, that of domination by hegemony.'

Ideological commitment and a normative orientation to the organisation means that workers, particularly key workers, are not pitting an alternative set of interests against the organisation. Indeed the work of people like Mayo and the Human Relations movement was just about getting workers to harmonise with the organisation, to develop social solidarity with the enterprise through rules which have been described as 'socio-regulative' or normative. Mayo attempted 'to restore hegemonic domination without resort to the coercive aspect of unemployment' by developing new forms of social solidarity to replace those destroyed by the industrial process of de-skilling (Clegg 1979, p.132). Nevertheless, control and power, though humanised, remain clearly with the owners and managers. The underlying structure of social relationships and the domination of managerial designs over worker's behaviour remains essentially intact.

Friedman (1977) has suggested that technical rules and de-skilling are applied to workers who are more peripheral to the labour process while socio-regulative rules will tend to be applied to those workers who are more central to the labour process. Those workers who possess special skills and understandings that cannot be rationalised and therefore controlled by technical means can only be controlled 'hegemonically' or normatively.

All this leads Clegg to say that power in organisations is expressed through the control of the means and methods of production. Power, then, 'when it is exercised is exercised over issues' (Clegg 1979, p.146). A critical issue will be one 'which affects organisational control of the labour process <u>within the context of the hegemonic domination of the ground rules (the objective organising principle) in which the organisation labours</u>' (Clegg 1979, p.146, emphasis original). Following this is the important corollary that <u>power will be exercised to reassert control</u>. It is only when managerial ideologies fail and the normative control they represent slips, when 'assumptions fail, routines lapse and "problems" appear that the overt exercise of power is necessary' (Clegg 1979, p.147). Pfeffer (1981, p.76) notes that when there is technological uncertainty, power in the form of management decree is more likely to determine whatever decisions are made. When there is no appeal available to a commonly held discipline or technology, decisions are informed by non-technical rulings. Organisational authority or administrative criteria are asserted. Whereas private sector organisations agree that profit maximisation is the agreed goal, matters are exacerbated in many public sector organisations where there may not even be agreement over aims never mind the techniques to achieve them.

Thus, the most effective exercise of power is the ability to set the ideological climate in which the very thoughts and actions of workers are shaped and expressed. In this way resistance and conflict do not even arise. The most insidious exercise of power is to prevent people 'from having grievances by shaping their perceptions, cognitions and preferences' (Lukes 1974, p.24). Nevertheless, the arrangement of ideas and practice favour the interests of certain groups (managers) against others (workers) (Walsh et al. 1981). Only when workers are threatening to break out of this 'ideological hegemony' do we see more primitive forms of power being expressed through coercion and command. Occupational groups who are in a position either to recognise or question the nature of managerial control and definition represent a problem which if it cannot be solved by normative 'incorporation' may result in either a shift in organisational power or a rejection of that occupational group's role in the organisation. In this way occupational groups tackling critical issues and formulating responses may, according to Allen (1975, pp.218-247):

(i) do so within the understanding and accepted methods of the organisation and its managers. They frame their responses within the dominant theorising power in order for them to be ruled admissible;

(ii) or attempt to formulate issues in terms outside the prevailing framework of understanding promulgated by management. This is a <u>radical</u> position insofar as it asserts that current patterns of thought and action are the product of those in control and that things could be understood otherwise. The success of the radical position depends on other powerful interest groups backing the alternative understanding thereby setting up competition over who controls the work. This is a clear reminder that organisational control is not a matter which can be understood simply within terms of the organisation itself but links it with wider societal interests and arrangements of power. Salaman (1978, p.519) maintains that 'organisational power and control must be seen in terms of the nature and priorities of the "host" society rather than as consequences of the particular forms of work process or technology' and that there is a 'relationship between internal organisational structures, processes and ideologies and the society within which they exist'.

SUMMARY OF CONCEPTS

Several ideas and concepts emerge from this selective review of the literature on the sociology of organisations and work. Many of the authors reviewed are categorised as 'radical structuralists' by Burrell and Morgan (1979). From this standpoint, organisations are understood in a wider social, political and economic context in which various interests are asserted. The social significance and structure of an organisation arises out of its location within society's network of power relations. 'From the radical Weberian standpoint it is the issue of power which stands at the centre of the analytical stage' (Burrell and Morgan 1979, p.376). Moreover, there is particular interest in the ways which the state and its concerns influence the social structures around it. Interests are seen to vary. Conflict is seen as endemic. And power is regarded as integral but unequally distributed throughout organisations with ruling interest groups exercising their power through various forms of ideological manipulation as well as displays of overt authority.

There is the argument that those who do well in the competition over who controls the content and direction of work are able to define the organisation, its environment and technology. They achieve a degree of power vis-a-vis other occupational groups. When 'hegemonic' control is incomplete or unsuccessful, 'weaker' groups are able to resist, express conflict or pose alternative understandings. These may lead to more direct technical or legal authoritative forms of control being asserted by more powerful occupational groups as they attempt to maintain their interests.

8 Professional control

Hughes points out that professionals profess. 'They profess to know better than others the nature of certain matters, and to know better than their clients what ails them or their affairs. This is the essence of the professional idea and the professional claim.' (Hughes 1971, p.375). Collectively, professionals 'presume to tell society what is good and right for the individual and for society at large in some aspect of life. Indeed, they set the very terms in which people may think about this aspect of life.' (Hughes 1958, p.79). Hughes described professionals as having a licence to carry out their brand of practice in vital areas in exchange for money, goods and services. Further, the more successful professions also claim a mandate to define what is proper conduct with respect to matters concerning their work, and so limit the rights of others to comment and act within their professional province (Hughes 1971, p.287). However different 'professional' groups differ in their ability to have others see things their way.

Johnson took the analysis of the professions a major stage further by arguing that the functionalist account 'is a distortion of reality because it neglects a historical explanation which indicates that any given reward structure is the result of arrogation by groups with the power to secure their claims and create their own system of legitimation' (Johnson 1972, p.37). Similarly, Rueschmeyer (1964, 1973), in examining the legal profession, also offered an early example which rejects notions of professional selflessness. Complex societies codify their rules of social life and employ sanctions to make sure that they are followed. Experts then become necessary; they know about, understand and apply these rules. Since rules are critical to the operations of all societies, the occupation which specialises in legal rules occupies a central and powerful position in community life. Reuschmeyer notes that law does not have a scientific body of knowledge, but it is based on the technical delivery of normative assessments, comments and information. Norms and central values are not equally held by all members of society, nor are they of equal relevance to all. Accordingly, in practising the law some interests are supported more favourably than others. As the nature of the lawyers task is to become an expert in what is legitimately possible and as the rules are set by the most powerful, lawyers, in serving the interests of the strong, are rewarded with the freedom, mandate and virtual monopoly to operate within a highly busy, central and remunerative area of social life.

In Marxist analyses, central values and established norms are nothing more than the dominant values and ruling norms of society's powerful people. Those who support and conform to norms are rewarded while deviants are punished. This means that the person who will be most favourably placed in society is the person who best succeeds in adapting to the ruling norms. It is in this manner that society rewards the conformity that sustains it.

The success of the established professions is based on their ability to gain and expand their control over key areas of everyday life which have become critical to the maintenance of the social structure, particularly when such uncertainties and irregularities do not lend themselves to obvious and routine practices. If the occupation can create skills and expertise in which it is not possible, by their nature or by law, for others to engage without themselves becoming members of the occupation and these skills are not normally available to the lay public, the occupation can distance itself from its clients. Intervention by outsiders is not easily achieved, leaving the occupation in prime control of its own practices. Professions are seen as a form of domination by technology (Illich 1977). Understanding the professions solely in terms of their self-proclaimed attributes fails to take account of the historical conditions in which groups of specialists attempt to establish a monopoly over specific tasks within the division of labour. The history of the professions is a story of collective mobility to gain control over crucial interests in the fields of health, justice and general welfare (see Johnson 1973).

Not that the story is destined to remain simple, for once

having gained occupational power, the professions themselves become a force with which to be reckoned. Indeed, Johnson in his later work goes on to argue that the formation of the modern western state is closely tied to the development of the professions (Johnson 1982). The first observers of the professions confused the appearance with the substance. This misled many of the theoreticians of would-be professions like social work (Flexner 1915; Greenwood 1965; Toren 1972). The eagerness with which the aspiring professions tried to acquire the trappings of professionalism was soon followed by their failure to look like and pass as the real thing. They had not recognised the more politically robust character of the established professions, particularly as they related to the social and political structures of society itself.

THE PROFESSIONS AND POWER

There are many people who believe they have the best answers to what troubles individuals and society, but only a few will win through and have most of us see things their way. Professions, said Illich (1977, p.16), not only determine how work should be done and by whom (the producers) but also they decide what services shall be produced and for whom (the consumers).

Johnson (1972) was one of the first to explore the relationship between producers and consumers, practitioners and clients, particularly in those occupations which have become known as the professions. He felt that the nature of the service on offer and the power relations that existed between consumer and producer would determine whether uncertainty was reduced at the expense of either the producer or the consumer. This in turn would lead to more or less power and autonomy accruing to the occupation. Practitioners who could increase their social distance from the client, because their skill was particularly valued but not easily understood, could increase their autonomy and control over their own practices. Medicine, for example, handles particularly acute problems of uncertainty, where client or consumer judgement is ineffective and the seeking of skilled help necessarily invites intrusion into intimate and vulnerable areas of the consumer's identity. The 'helplessness' of the consumer in situations such as these increases uncertainty. The relative 'weakness' of the patient in this relationship gives the power to the practitioner and the uncertainty is resolved in the manner of the practitioner's choosing and to his benefit.

Social work, on the other hand, has not convinced its public that it possesses skills which are either highly valued or difficult to understand. Consumers, including clients, courts, the public and the state, feel a certain amount of familiarity and knowledge about the things with which social workers deal and so feel able to assume a more dominant position in the producer-consumer relationship. Because social work arises in response to the problems of everyday living, its expertise rests in gaining a thorough and sensitive understanding of ordinary matters. The catch for social workers is that if the technical base and strength of an occupation consists of a vocabulary that sounds familiar to everyone it will have difficulty in claiming a monopoly of skill or even a roughly exclusive jurisdiction over its working environment. To the onlooker, the practices of social workers do not appear markedly different from those of ordinary social intercourse (Nokes 1967, p.x). The profession does not appear to possess much in the way of an esoteric technology. To the lay public, which includes state politicians and legislators, there is an unwillingness to 'recognise the need for special competence in an area where everyone is an "expert"' (Wilensky 1962). There is not a great willingness or apparent need to hand over occupational control to social workers, and as social workers are not felt to hold either rare or vital skills, the balance of power remains with the community.

So, asks Wilding (1982, p.9), 'How does an occupational group gain a privileged position in society?' or 'Why does the state grant a range of privileges and accept a loss of power to a particular occupational group?'. Certainly expertise is involved, but so too 'are other factors - the power of the group, the compatability of its interests with the interests of powerful groups in society, the measure of support which the group has from wider public opinion'. Professionalism, according to Johnson (1972, p.45), can now be defined 'as a peculiar type of occupational control rather than an expression of the inherent nature of particular occupations. A profession is not, then, an occupation but a means of controlling an occupation'. A profession 'has been given the right to control its own work' (Freidson 1970, p.71). And for Larson (1977 and 1979), professionalisation amounts to a 'project' to gain market control over both the product (expert acts) and the production of the professionals themselves. Professionalisation is a process by which producers of special services seek 'to constitute and control a market for their expertise' (Larson 1977, p.xvi).

Wilding (1982, p.6) says that above all, professionals want autonomy and control of their own terms of work. 'To this end are claims for the exclusion of the uninitiated, control of entry, and licensing of members directed ... The supposed characteristics of professions - service ethic, length of training, and so on can all then be regarded as links in the chain of argument directed to that end, rather than as inherent and inalienable characteristics of the work of particular occupations - in short as attempts at gaining and justifying power and privilege' (Wilding 1982, p.6).

JOHNSON'S TYPOLOGY

In 1972, Johnson described three types of institutional control which he saw as resolving the tensions that existed in the producer-consumer relationship:

1. <u>Colleague or collegiate control</u>, in which the producer dominates the relationship with the client. This is the 'professionalism' traditionally associated with law and medicine. Here, the producer defines the needs of the consumer <u>and</u> the manner in which these needs are catered for. Fundamental to the power of the professions in policy making and administration is an acceptance of their right to define needs and problems as well as answers and resources. The demand for the skills of the practitioner coupled with their meeting diverse, basic and unorganised interests allows the occupation to establish authoritative control over its own workings.

2. <u>Client control</u>, in which the consumer has the power to define his own needs and the manner in which they are to be met. In effect, the consumer institutes a form of patronage, 'keeping' the practitioner and his skills for his own exclusive use. Aristrocratic patrons maintained artists, architects and doctors in this fashion. Today, accountants, working for large corporate organisations, by and large have their activities determined by their employer.

3. <u>Third party control</u>, in which an outside individual or body <u>mediates</u> in the relationship between practitioner and client. The third party defines both the needs <u>and</u> the manner in which the needs are to be met. State mediation is perhaps the most widespread instance of this type of control. For example, welfare state activities define who are to be seen as clients and outline what kind of responses they are to expect. Social workers regularly find themselves operating within a predefined context, but increasingly practitioners in other occupations experience similar limitations placed around their practice as the state increases its responsibilities, powers and say in the services provided. Larson (1977, pp.181-82), too, notes that social workers have their clients and demands for their services guaranteed, especially as the turn of the century witnessed the shift from voluntary welfare work to 'a form of urban social control based upon formalised methods'.

DEFINING THE PROBLEM AND THE RESPONSE

Uncertainty, then, cannot be dealt with in just any way. The manner of its resolution is as important as the fact that it can be done. The radical redistribution of wealth may be the way to improve the health of working-class old people or the social conduct of the poor, but any occupation that regularly preaches this as the answer is liable to lose not only its credibility but the ability to control its own affairs. Occupations with high discretionary roles gain privileges because their activities implicitly confirm and promote what is valued by the organisation and society. Perrow (1972, p.69) puts it more sharply:

> The less the expertise, the more direct the surveillance, and the more obtrusive the controls. The more the expertise, the more unobtrusive the controls. The best situation of all, though they do not come cheap, is to hire professionals, for someone else has socialized them and even unobtrusive controls are hardly needed. The professional, the prima donna of organizational theory, is really the ultimate eunuch - capable of doing everything well in that harem except that which he should not do, and in this case that is to mess around with the goals of the organization, or the assumptions that determine to what ends he will use his professional skills.

Many of medicine's harshest critics, for example, see it linked closely in its outlook and practices to an economic order which relies on inequalities. Medicine is reluctant to concede that many of its concerns are as much to do with inequalities of wealth, housing, diet and environment as individuals whose bodies are not working too well. Individual failure, pathology and unfitness (temporary or permanent) to be a useful member of society underlie conceptions of disease, illhealth and sickness. Amongst the disabling characteristics associated with professionals' defining need, according to McKnight (1977) is the practice of placing the perceived deficiency in the client. 'While most modernised professionals will agree that individual problems develop in a socio-economic-political context ... Because his remedial tools and techniques are usually limited to individualised interaction, the interpretation of the need becomes individualised. The tool defines the problem rather than the problem defining the tool' (McKnight 1977, p.79). Medicine has been granted a monopoly in officially defining illness and health. In developing practices, a knowledge and attitude to people and their bodies, medicine has constructed and monopolised large areas of uncertainty. The result is that medicine has achieved a powerful control over its own activities and those of others (Alford

1975; Ham 1982).

Law, too, has managed to ally itself with prevailing standards but on the surface appears unlike medicine. The lawyer's knowledge is not scientific, nor concerned with predicting or explaining events on the basis of natural laws. Rather, it is concerned with a body of social norms and with rules for their application. By his very practice the lawyer confirms the existing social order. His is a 'normative' practice and therefore contains a large element of indetermination which, over the centuries, has been left in the control of the legal profession. As Rueschmeyer (1973, p.16) says, the competent lawyer both needs to know the law and grasp the social context enabling him to 'define situations'. Lawyers peddle the language of the law. 'Lawyers coerce the experiences and life situations of their clients to fit their definitions. Lawyers are responsible for individualising and depoliticising issues. This is inevitable if an issue is to be constituted in terms of legal discourse' (Cain 1979, p.109).

Professions generate ideologies out of their cognitive and normative resources which allow them to 'construct particular areas of social reality' (Larson 1977, p.xiii). In this sense, 'all professionals are priests; they interpret mysteries which affect the lives of those who do not understand' (Sennett quoted in Larson 1977, p.31). But occupations whose 'professional project' has not given them strong 'market control' remain relatively weak in their ability to define the outlook and content of their own practice. Their interpretations of 'life's mysteries' receive little more value than those of others. Indeed other occupational groups, such as organisation managers, may assert their views of the situation in direct competition. Their success not only thwarts professional strategies but weakens the would-be profession's ability to resist managers' efforts to 'decompose' professional tasks into more routine, less expert acts. In this way professional projects can be suppressed and depressed.

CONCLUSIONS

Recent work on the professions sees their occupational strengths grounded in the power resources that different groups derive from their position in the division of labour (Rueschmeyer 1983, p.44). When successful, the professional project brings control over a range of important areas including practice, organisation and resources. Thus, occupations which are described as professional appear to have gained control over the content of their own practice. The strongest professions are able to define both the nature of the problems which come their way and the type of response deemed most appropriate.

Few professions stop short at just controlling the content of their work. Professional groups go on to press for control over the organisation of work. They seek control over resource allocation. Professionals can determine the way their service operates, particularly in terms of where resources are concentrated and which 'consumers' and which 'professional skills' receive resource backing. Professionals do not simply usurp political decision-making; they create the actual terms in which policies and plans are to be understood (Wilding 1982).

9 Controlling the meaning of welfare work

The previous three chapters identified a number of concepts which can be used to understand the organisation of workers and their work in the personal social services:

1. Control over the nature and definition of the work.
2. Control over the content of work.
3. Control over the organisation of work and workers.
4. The power that derives from such control.
5. The potential conflict that exists between the occupational groups competing to achieve control over the content of practice.

These ideas and concepts offer the prospect of a common explanatory base to a range of phenomena, including the distribution and differentiation of social workers and their practice and the response patterns within particular cases. The explanation, as it is developed, begins to encompass ideas concerning the nature of social work and its organisation. In this way, links are made within the same conceptual schema between (i) the work, (ii) the occupational groups that tackle the work and (iii) the relationship between these groups including their organisation.

What takes place in the politics of occupational control is not entirely divorced from what takes place in a fieldworker's practice. Examining social work case practice with reference only to 'professional' social work concepts frustrates the making of wider links between social work practice and the organisation of social workers. Instead of seeing the organisation of social workers as an unfortunate constraint on practice, the organisation of social workers can be seen as a higher level form arising out of the same conceptual ingredients that occur at the 'micro level' of individual practice. Explicit in such an explanation is the view that social work and those who 'claim' it as their 'professional' concern are not the sole arbiters of what is 'best' or 'right' in the name of social work. Rather, definitions of practice emerge out of the competing views of different occupational and interest groups (cf Glastonbury et al. 1980, p.26).

This view of welfare occupations and their work suggests that social work practice does not have inherent qualities that allow universal definitions to be made, that social work has no essential nature just waiting to be expressed by that occupational group which believes itself to be in a position to pronounce on the true nature of the job. Fieldworkers and welfare managers represent two occupational groups which have employed different strategies to establish control over the work done and so have things seen their way in the light of their concerns. Out of the relationship between these alternative strategies and their different 'technological' bases arises the design of work, the division of labour, the style of technology used, the structure of the organisation and the definition of the 'raw material' (clients, their needs and their problems).

SEQUENCE OF INTERPRETATION

It is within the work carried out on individual cases (Chapter 5) that the basic elements which characterise the relationship between occupational control and the content of practice are discovered. The identification of this basic relationship not only helps explain the distribution of types of response present in particular cases, but also can be used to account for a broader range of phenomena, including the 'activity profiles' (Chapter 4) and the general distribution of fieldworkers and their work (Chapter 2). The explanations offered in Chapter 3 are now superseded and subsumed by the more encompassing theoretical accounts described in Chapters 6, 7 and 8. The interpretation of the results is presented in the following order:

1. Types of response in particular kinds of cases (interpreting the results of Chapter 5).
2. The pattern of responses and their evolution within and between cases (continuing the interpretation of

the results of Chapter 5).
3. The distribution of activities amongst fieldworkers and client groups (interpreting the results of Chapter 4).
4. The distribution and differentiation of fieldworkers and their client groups (interpreting the results of Chapter 2).

1. TYPES OF RESPONSE IN PARTICULAR KINDS OF CASES

In their handling of particular cases, fieldworkers perceive and understand their work and then respond in a variety of ways. The freedoms and constraints experienced or recognised in these acts of perception, understanding and response tell us something about the amount of control fieldworkers appear to enjoy or lack over their work. The perceptions and understandings reached are stimulated either by professional and personal theories about practice or by organisational and administrative requirements. Control over the content of a piece of practice is therefore rooted in either professional assertions or managerial designs. Control, from the social workers' point of view, may be more or less available along two dimensions:

(i) Control over the 'raw material' itself; that is the extent to which the worker's skills and occupational technology can have a predictable effect on clients and their problems.
(ii) Control over the way clients are perceived and understood and the responses offered in the light of these; that is the extent to which the social worker's responses are prescribed and shaped by either the individual worker ('professional' control) or others, particularly managers, either directly (centralised management control) or indirectly (formalised management control).

The amount of control experienced or credited to social workers allows us to say something about their occupation and the nature of its practice. The results of the taped interviews (Chapter 5) might now be interpreted around whether or not the two dimensions of control are present or absence in particular areas of fieldwork practice. Thus the following positions are theoretically available to fieldworkers:

1. The fieldworker experiences personal control over the content of her work ('professional' control) including:
    (i) the 'raw materials', that is the people, events and circumstances that make up cases;
    (ii) the responses made in working with a case (non-programmed and so at the worker's discretion).

2. The fieldworker does <u>not</u> experience personal control over the content of her work including:
    (i) the behaviour of the 'raw materials';
    (ii) the responses made in working with a case because of either organisational constraints of structure, design, rules and resources (formalised management control), or explicit directives by managers (centralised management control).

The recognition of strengths and weaknesses in the amount of control held by fieldworkers over the elements of practice offers a clear insight into the occupational standing of social workers. If control is weak over both the 'raw materials' and the the responses made in practice, social workers are unlikely to have work defined to suit their occupational skills or to develop organisations which confer control and power on their occupation. Mapping the contours of control in practice reveals where the balance of power lies between the worker and the managers of her agency. The results of Chapter 5 do just this, and it now remains to describe the occupational relief as it exists between field social workers and their managers in more pronounced terms.

The results show that the two major dimensions of control over the content of practice generally were weak in the case of field social workers. The occupational skills and techniques of the worker, although attempted frequently as non-programmed responses, generally failed to bring people and their situations under sufficient control. In the event of such failure, the more restricted strategies of managers and administrators were employed. The use of formal procedures and statutory devices allowed situations to be viewed more narrowly and in this narrow sense, control could be achieved more easily. The responses, though, are not of the worker's own manufacture. Formally programmed responses had a high occurrence across all client groups, suggesting that managerial control was prevalent and pervasive. The effect of such weakness is that fieldworkers are subjected to control from elsewhere - either by the momentum of case evolution (the 'raw material' goes its own way) and/or through the determination of responses by managers effected through the division of labour, resource provision, procedure and directives. There might also be an element of 'managers knowing best' - a form of collective disillusion with the claims of professionalism, an organisational recognition that formal procedures are the proven 'best way' of making a minimally acceptable response.

There is, of course, a close relationship between the weakness of social workers' expertise and the strong control exerted by managers. In terms of asserting the claim to control and define the nature of the work, managers and social workers represent two different occupational strategies. Each makes use of a different technological base. Indeed the techniques, as means, are used to different ends. The 'professional' end and means have had less success in welfare work than those employed by managers. As Pearson (1975, p.56) puts it, the social worker 'even at the most basic level of performance - immediate client response ... cannot say confidently that if he does A he will 'cause' B to follow'. In similar vein, one of my respondents reflected:

> I don't actually think I bring about particular changes; through what I do I mean, like stopping Gary pinching things. I mean, I try. I go through all the recommended motions and he may stop or he may not. So far he hasn't! I just hang in.

And in work with the elderly, Goldberg and Warburton observed (1979, p.94): 'In over two-thirds of the cases for whom a continuance of domiciliary services and occasional surveillance was prescribed, unanticipated events outside the control of social workers intervened before the next review.'

The effect of management-based techniques gaining control is not just that control by social workers is reduced but that the content of the work is prescribed both explicitly (through authority-based directives) and implicitly (by managerial design and structure). Explicit and implicit controls occur across all areas of work, but actual mixes and distributions vary most between work with children and their families on the one hand and work with the old and frail on the other.

Direct and usually explicit managerial involvement in fieldwork practice was most common in child care and family work. This was particularly so when the behaviour and circumstances of individuals were clearly related to the statutory responsibilities of the agency. In critical situations the worker's discretion was curtailed with more direct reference being made to statute, policy, procedure and managerial authority. Discretion, particularly over the methods used, was greatest in situations where the outcome was not critically the concern of the agency or where matters, as currently understood, were not likely to present the organisation with too much uncertainty in terms of its responsibilities. As one fieldworker put it, referring to his use of family therapy as a technique of working:

> My Area Officer doesn't care about the way I do it, so long as I do it, so long as I'm in there and can say I'm in there.

In these cases, although allowed to behave in ways based on their own technology and expertise, fieldworkers essentially were indicating to the department that they were involved and alert to what was happening. That the departments, in some cases at least, did not mind how the workers conducted the manner of their involvement is captured in the rueful remarks of this young and recently qualified woman:

> I was told by our Area Officer that I couldn't go on the course (week long family therapy workshop). I'm really interested in family work and see it ... well as a really useful way of handling many of my cases, you know. He said he was sorry, but really if I wanted to specialise in that type of work I would be better off in a specialist agency of some kind. It was a luxury that we couldn't afford at area team level. I ask you!

If clients did begin to exhibit features which the organisation felt to be of direct relevance to its operations, the discretionary control allowed social workers was withdrawn. The case was then placed within the tighter framework of managerial authority and design. So, for example, when teenagers committed offences or parents were suspected of being a danger to their children, the responses of the fieldworker obeyed either procedural guidelines or the directives of managers. Cooper (in Glastonbury et al. 1980, p.78) observed that in one SSD, when making child care decisions 'at least four tiers in the department were recorded as involved' with a tendency to view decision making as concentrated in the hands of the committee and management. In critical areas of child care the worker loses control over the content of her own practice and follows the practice designs of other people.

Parton (1979 and 1981) has considered similar influences at work in child care practice with cases of suspected non-accidental injury. He examines the growing concern and anxiety surrounding the recognition of child abuse. He relates the establishment of child abuse as a problem and the 'moral panic' it has engendered 'to certain influential economic interests and the changing ideological and material base of British society' (1981, p.394). In the 1970s the family, as an institution, was felt to be 'at risk', a 'victim' of 1960s permissiveness. The feeling that 'something should be done' developed. Parton quotes (1981, p.393) an article from the Sunday Times, 11th November 1973, which argues that baby battering 'rightly horrifies the public and it is a category where society is failing to do its duty ... the tragedy of Maria Colwell deserves attention because her death dramatises a national scandal.' Rather than see families as 'neglectful' or 'inadequate' as tended to be the case in the 1950s and 1960s, they came to be seen as violent and deviant allowing formal social control to be the proper reaction in which intervention was more likely to be coercive and authoritative. The way the problem was being conceptualised and the way priorities were set, increasingly influenced the DHSS and the advice it gave SSDs. In turn this affected the working definitions and practices of managers and fieldworkers.

In this climate, both deviant families and the permissive practices of social workers could be controlled and disciplined. 'The moral panic related to child abuse has been inextricably interrelated with debates about the nature and direction of social work and the accountability of social workers ... It is now the major concern of the practitioners and their employing departments' (Parton 1981, p.406). Social workers became forced into a more coercive relationship with a large number of families. Their practice, as Holman (1976) has argued, has legitimately been encouraged to be more punitive, interventive and 'rescue' minded. Parton (1981, p.407) quotes Jordan on the changing role of the social worker:

> It is much more linked to the task of investigating and acting upon allegations of neglect and ill-treatment of children, which after all was one of the duties of the local authority social worker; this now suddenly looms much larger and sets the tone of all other work with 'at risk' children - 'at risk' comes to mean 'at risk from parents' rather than 'at risk of coming into care' ... social workers are increasingly exhorted to act as rescuers, saving children from wicked or feckless parents.

Social work practice in child care and family work is not left simply to the professional discretion of the worker. The worker's understanding of individual cases and the responses she makes are outcomes of 'wider social processes', structural developments and the role of the state (Parton 1981, pp.409-410). 'The panic over child abuse has biased departmental priorities, caseloads and professional practice in terms of child and family problems. Such a bias now seems to be accepted as natural by those in the field' (Parton 1981, p.409).

The net result of increased surveillance and direct control of certain families according to Parton is 'that the removal of a child from its parents is now seen far more as a first rather than a last resort' (1983, p.392). Between March 1972 and March 1976 there was nearly a fourfold increase in the number of Place of Safety Orders taken (204 to 759). And whereas only one newborn child was compulsorily placed in care out of 81 departments who returned evidence in 1970, the same departments reported 42 such removals in 1978 (Parton 1981, pp.392-393).

Examination of DHSS returns reveals a 27% increase in the number of children for whom parental rights have been assumed between 1976 and 1979, the number growing from 14,500 to 18,400. By 1980, some 41% of the children in voluntary care in England and Wales were subject to parental rights resolutions. Social work practice clearly does not operate in a social, political or occupational vacuum.

Implicit methods of control were met in practice with all client groups. However, work with the old and the handicapped was particularly liable to indirect methods of control and prescription. Again, fieldworkers <u>in situ</u> had considerable discretion over the manner of their responses. Their actions were not determined in exact detail. Nevertheless, the worker's perception of clients and the way their needs were recognised and understood was set within the framework laid down by the organisation and its managers. Clients were viewed as individuals whose needs could be recognised and met in terms of the resources available; they were approached for information which would determine their eligibility for existing services.

Lee (1982, p.30), describing social workers' adoption of managerially designed systems of practice and accountability, sees the work increasingly subject to 'technicalisation and routine de-skilling'. Bamford (1982, p.38), in his book addressed to managers in social work, notes the use of 'Operational Priority Systems' in SSDs which 'give managers additional means of controlling the flow of work' as well as viewing available responses from the perspectives of the agency. One of my interviewees, a qualified social worker, found her work prescribed and her outlooks limited in a case involving a young man who was physically handicapped even though she believed she could see other needs and methods of working:

> The agency ... doesn't allow you a lot of time to do a lot of personal counselling in cases like this. You're more of a resource system, a getter and provider of a limited range of resources and this is how I'm supposed basically to tackle this case. But really, if I could I would like to do some counselling with Peter's mother.

A telephone survey conducted by Neill (1982) looked at the procedures and criteria related to Part III applications in the 33 local authorities throughout the GLC area in the autumn of 1977. Although there were variations in the way Part III applications were defined, the study indicates a relationship between case practice, the decision making process and 'the powerful and important needs and politics of organisations' (p.241). The part that managers played in determining eligibility and priority were seen both in the provision of resources (the number of Part III beds available) and the tendency for final decisions to be taken centrally in many authorities:

> In two-thirds (21) of authorities, two systems of classification were in operation. Priority applicants were first selected by referring social workers in consultation with their senior colleagues in area office or hospital. These selected 'priority' applicants were then further screened by a central management person or panel ... In ten of the remaining boroughs all Part 3 applicants were classified at the central office, and priority applicants then selected by a panel or an individual. (Neill 1982, p.237)

There was a pressure on social workers to define their clients' situations in crisis terms in order to gain Part III places. Scarcity of resources, in this case, affected the assessments made. It also led to the organisation needing to control decisions by taking them centrally.

The results of Neill's research and other studies, suggest a common pattern in which clients are measured, using departmental formulae, to see to what extent they fit available services. The forms to be filled control and guide perceptions and responses. In this sense, social workers adopt a procrustean style of practice in which the basic design of services, including the routes to them and the gateways met on the way, is constructed by managers interpreting the legislation. Black et al. (1983) reached similar conclusions: in the provision of practical services 'delivery systems were overbureaucratised, governed less by individual needs than routinised procedure' (p.219) and 'for elderly people, problems were redefined to fit the available solutions of existing practical services' (p.222). In these ways managers control the content of many areas of fieldwork practice. It is further reflected in the division of labour in which there is an implicit acknowledgement that work with the old and handicapped contains a relatively high and unambiguous prescriptive component. Unqualified workers predominate in this area of work. Indeed the origins of social work assistants and welfare aides lie in the recruitment policies of SSDs in the early 1970s with managers seeking a growth in the number of workers to handle the old and disabled (Hey 1979).

2. THE DISTRIBUTION, OCCURRENCE AND EVOLUTION OF RESPONSES

The dissolution of independent 'professional' types of control, which assert a social work technology, into responses which reflect managerially inspired understandings receives further confirmation when the direction of dissolution is considered. If managerial technologies receive their characteristics and ultimately their strength from interpreting and administering statutes and society's expectations of personal service work, then two principal directions of dissolution might be anticipated:

(i) Child care legislation addresses itself to standards of behaviour exhibited by children and their parents. The work of SSDs involves surveillance, monitoring and controlling the welfare and conduct of children. The work is not described in terms of 'curing' or 'mending' faulty behaviour, but rather in terms of establishing guidelines and procedures about what responses should occur when certain behaviours are identified. Thus the responses in this area of work occur along a spectrum: independent responses within the worker's control dissolving into formally programmed and ultimately, in some cases, centrally controlled responses. It is to programmed responses that social workers turn or are directed when the conduct of clients brings them clearly into statutory focus in spite of the technical efforts of the 'professional' social worker.

(ii) Work with the old and handicapped rests on legislation which, in general terms, describes the services and resources these client groups might expect from local authorities. From the outset most workers adopt a 'service' outlook. This is set within a managerially designed framework of procedures, resources and responses.

In both major areas of practice - work with children and work with the old and handicapped - control shifted in favour of managers, though the overall complexion of control strategies differed in each case. Implicit control mechanisms allow routine, unreflective responses to occur for which there is no organisational need to employ independently skilled workers. Control is at its most potent when it is subtle and implicit, when workers do not even recognise that there might be other ways of understanding the work. In these situations there is no need for managers to display power overtly. This form of control ('ideological hegemony') is most prevalent in work with the old and handicapped.

Control in child care work is more visible and apparent. Behaviours are judged, laws invoked and procedures applied. Management and statutory determination are 'on the surface', partly because the work cannot be straightforwardly routinised and partly because the workers are required to assess the evidence on behalf of the agency which obliges the administration to reveal its hand by the overt invocation of legal standards, controls and directives. The fact that child care and family work appears more likely to contain examples of uncertainty which stubbornly remain outside the technical powers of both workers and managers (persistent offenders, absconders, families in chronic poverty, foster homes which break down) is a point which has to be borne in mind when considering the distribution and differentiation of workers and their practices. If neither occupational group's strategy can effect sufficient control over case practice, neither group can entirely determine the practice and occupational organisation of the other.

As argued, explicit control is a weaker power base than those founded on normative consensus. To the extent that power is weaker, there is some potential for workers to assert their own occupational control base. In certain situations, social workers recognise that they have an alternative view and understanding of the work. Even so, in SSDs the balance of control, even in the less predictable area of child care, lies with the managers although social workers have been able to explore pockets of freedom. The irony is that this less complete form of control in child care matters not only generates more examples of explicit disagreements between occupational groups but it also witnesses the overt use of power in the form of managerial directives. Managerial authority thus appears most blatant in those areas of work which are least under the detailed control of managers.

Conclusions on the types of responses appearing in case practice

Worker's control over:

'Raw materials'	Critical case responses	
+	+	Strong professional control/High worker discretion
−	+	Weak professional control/High worker discretion
+	−	Weak managerial control/Low worker discretion
−	−	Strong managerial control/Low worker discretion

Figure 9.1 Four occupational levels of control over the content of practice

Figure 9.1 summarises the positions theoretically available to field social workers. When the worker is able to control critical case responses and has high discretion over the content of practice, professional control is high. In the case of fieldwork practice in SSDs, the workers characteristically had little control over critical case responses and experienced low powers of discretion. This is not the stuff of professional control. And although managerial control was not uniformly strong, it nevertheless held the balance of power throughout all client group categories and was at its most subtle and pervasive in work with the old and disabled.

The meaning that different types of client group have for organisations and the responses expected in the light of these meanings are determined by managers as they interpret the agency's brief and role in the community. The effect of such control is to influence the content of fieldwork practice in far reaching and penetrating ways. As Smith and Ames (1976, p.52) remark, 'the way in which a department as a whole operates does crucially constrain both the way in which decisions are taken and the outcome of these decisions within area teams'.

3. ACTIVITY AND PROBLEM PROFILES

Statistical profiles were tabled for the range and type of problems and activities associated with different types of fieldworker and client group (see Chapter 4). Problem and activity profiles were found to be (i) different between client groups, but (ii) similar for different kinds of fieldworker working with the same client group. In the conclusions to these results, this state of affairs was taken to indicate that the characteristics of the client group determined the type of work carried out irrespective of the kind of fieldworker. Fieldworkers appeared not to control the content of client group practice.

However, at this stage of interpretation, the introduction of the concepts culled from the sociological literature allows the 'profile' results to be interpreted within a deeper theoretical setting. Fundamentally, it is not the client group in itself which controls the content of worker practice. Rather, it is the way different client groups are perceived, understood and defined by those occupational groups able to describe the work in terms of their own outlook, interests and skills. SSD managers do not passively respond to their 'task environment'. They actively define it and shape it wherever possible so that it accords with their own abilities and resources. Client groups take on their meaning in the light of managerial interpretations and definitions.

Individual clients within particular client groups might display sufficient variation to disturb the original equation that 'the work determines the worker'. But under the present analysis, the similarity of problem and activity profiles by different kinds of worker for the same client group suggests that no matter what the individual case idiosyncracies might be, cases in the same client group, by and large, are perceived and handled uniformly.

Conversely, if fieldworkers using their occupational expertise were controlling the content of work ('the worker determines the work'), it might be expected that different types of fieldworker (qualified and unqualified, Level 1 and Level 3) working with the same client group would generate different 'profiles'. That this is not the case suggests that another mechanism controls the relationship between work and worker. Using the concept of occupational control, the formula 'work determines the worker' can be seen as merely the surface appearance of a deeper order.

Particular client groups are 'standardised' by the processing procedures and structures of the organisation. The idiosyncracies (intrinsic uncertainties) of individual clients are subdued or lost in the standardising process. The client group, as the organisation's 'raw material', is defined through statute, procedure, method of process and resources available. As interpreters of statute and designers of work, managers control the content of work. Their understanding penetrates the organisation and practice so that workers think and act in terms of the organisation's perceptions of the client groups. So although the definitions made of each client group vary, and so produce different profiles for each client group, different kinds of worker working within the same client group display similar 'profiles'.

Managers determine the meaning of each client group for the organisation and so determine the perceptions and responses of fieldworkers vis a vis each client group. One of Harris's (1979, p.71) respondents saw work with the elderly through the eyes of the organisation:

> I think that both in this office, and certainly in the one I was in before, it seems welfare work, by that I mean it's the term I use for work with the elderly, tended to be assigned pretty exclusively to welfare assistants and their brief is not to do casework. It is to do more, you know, mechanical jobs, in the sense of transportation, etc., and I think if the department says that welfare work is a fitting use of welfare assistants' time, then it may be saying something.

The organisation is also felt to influence the worker's

behaviour at early stages of involvement too. Addison (1982) sees the organisation determining work at the intake stage in an SSD as it attempts to defend itself against a range of anxieties, including the quantity of work, the insistence of events and the sense of impossibility, unpredictability and hostility in the environment. As well as what she sees as rational in the light of these demands, departments 'have to ration their services and set priorities in a formal way' (pp.615-16). The effect on the organisation and its workers is for them to perceive and understand the environment and clients in a particular way in order to reduce anxiety, minimise uncertainty and manage the work.

If the organisation influences the practices of workers, a certain commonality in approaches taken and activities conducted is to be expected. That there are more similarities than differences between social workers in practice has been realised by a number of authors who, like me, explain this state of affairs in terms of the structural boundaries that curtail and determine the content of practice (Bailey 1980; Black et al. 1983; Hardiker 1981, p.102). However, rather than just see the organisation as some inert, determining given, the present interpretation understands the organisation to be the product of particular occupational groups and their techniques and interests. In the case of SSDs it is managers who have largely devised the 'structural boundaries' that channel and predefine major elements of practice.

4. THE DISTRIBUTION AND DIFFERENTIATION OF FIELDWORKERS AND CLIENT GROUPS

On the face of it, the amount of indeterminacy and uncertainty confronting occupations which practise in the sphere of moral behaviour, social problems and human conduct is high. The opportunity for deciding how things are to be understood and how practitioners ought to proceed is considerable. But though people might try to explain delinquency or violence, the existence of such categories of behaviour depends upon moral and social judgements being made about those types of behaviour. Such matters cannot be derived from scientific theories (Downie and Loudfoot 1978; Hesse 1978). Communities react to the behaviour of their members and thus are responsible for designating the conduct of some individuals as unacceptable, anti-social and not to be tolerated. The premise that underlies all social work practice is that clients are clients, not because of any innate condition, but because society defines them as such (Davies, M. 1981; Howe 1979; Warham 1977). Ultimately, social workers have no mandate to define their clientele. In controlling how we understand and respond to departures from 'normal' and 'proper' moral and social behaviour, the 'ideological basis of indetermination' simply are not available to social workers for the purpose of occupational control (Johnson 1977, p.108). The state, as third party, mediates between practitioner and client. However, there are two areas in personal social service work over which occupational groups might establish some control:

   (i) the type of work and client group, with some areas being regarded as more critical or sensitive than others;

  (ii) the techniques and procedures available in order to cope with the work, particularly in areas where satisfactory or appropriate outcomes are not easily guaranteed.

Given these prospects, different client groups might be assessed in terms of the uncertainty which they are defined as displaying, their social importance and their susceptibility to particular types of occupational techniques and skills. Each client group offers a type of work which provides more or less opportunity for different occupational groups to increase their control over the content of practice. The distribution and differentiation of fieldworkers can now be explained with reference to the locus of control as it occurs between managers and fieldworkers, particularly as it affects the meaning given to each client group. The way client groups are defined and the meanings given to them by different occupational groups influences both the practices defined as appropriate and the type of worker allocated to that client group.

Again, the explanations offered in Chapter 3 are not entirely redundant. Rather, they are put in a broader context. Qualified social workers do 'ditch their dirty work'; the old and handicapped are delegated to lower ranked workers. But the reasons for such rejection lie less in the intrinsic unsuitability of the work for the expertise of qualified workers and more in the ability of managers to control exactly the meaning that such client groups have for the organisation and its resources. So it is that the work associated with the old and disabled becomes standardised and routine, with little need or opportunity for the use of discretion by workers. The association between certain types of worker and kinds of work can now be considered in terms of the balance of control over the meaning and content of practice as it occurs between managers and fieldworkers. The two major client groupings, the old and handicapped and children and their families, will be discussed in the light of this conceptual framework.

The old, physically and mentally handicapped

Legislation and policy affecting some client groups permits a relatively straightforward interpretation of the 'meaning' given to people and their problems, at least as it affects the agency, its organisation and services. Intrinsic uncertainties are 'defined out' by the limits of statutory interest and their organisational interpretation. If it is possible to deploy resources in a predictable, prescriptive and routine fashion in defined circumstances, control rests with those who design the service and not with those who carry it out. This is why formally programmed 'service' responses predominate in work with the old and handicapped.

'Professional' social work's technologies are inappropriate as far as the agency is concerned for much of the work with the old and handicapped because it only requires simple organisational responses in order to achieve the desired result. Therefore in terms of social workers gaining control over the content of practice, there is little potential in work with the old and handicapped. Management techniques are more suitable, sufficient and effective. There is no requirement to see or understand the work in more complex terms. Moreover, because the overriding condition of old people and the handicapped remains unalterable and therefore certain, there is no gain to be found in having other occupational groups define the work associated with these client groups. They remain old and handicapped. In which case there is no need to hand over control to other occupational groups working in these areas. Indeed all that is required of workers is that they follow procedures matching defined resources to defined need. So, as Larson (1977, p.222) says, 'In most occupations, routinised specialities tend to be the equivalent to the 'dirty work' which professions delegate to ancillary occupations'.

Children and their families

Whereas the legislation and its interpretation affecting old people and the handicapped permits a set of responses which can be adequately described by the provision of services and procedures, child care and family legislation requires a different interpretation. The 'raw material' of abusing parents and delinquent teenagers is perceived and understood to have greater intrinsic complexity and uncertainty. 'Doing something about' these behaviours is not so easily achieved. The two main and contrasting technologies available are those of control and cure, where control means either separating people (children from violent parents) or removing them (offenders from the community). Each offers the prospect of rendering the material stable and certain, but using a different set of techniques.

Control-based strategies remove or separate those who misbehave from those who suffer the consequences of their misbehaviour. In this way, the offending behaviour is said to be no longer possible. The new statutory situation offers 'certainty' in respect of the client suffering the behaviour as originally identified. For example, parents cannot assault their children or teenagers commit offences when they are no longer in the community. Although these situations bring immediate relief, the long term outcome is much less certain. Confidence in this line of action is not absolute. When children are encouraged to be reunited with their parents or delinquents returned to the community there is no guarantee that things will be better.

Cure techniques attempt to change the behaviour and attitudes of those 'malfunctioning' so that the offending behaviours and attitudes are eliminated. This holds the possibility of a more lasting resolution of the problem as defined by the law, the community and their agents. However the technology which backs this type of occupational practice is weak and as yet there is no guarantee that the outcome prescribed will be achieved. So, although cure poses the possibility of treating people so that their unacceptable behaviours are eliminated (which makes it a potentially attractive technology), its weaknesses mean that administrative and statutory control techniques, though not addressing the root causes, nevertheless have a short to medium term effect on reducing uncertainty, albeit in restricted terms.

Child care and family work has to be understood in such a way that neither 'professional' nor managerial technologies entirely get to grips with the main features of the work. Both have only a partial, temporary or some might say pyrrhic success in reducing uncertainty. The prospect of increasing occupational control over the content of practice in child care work is still open to social workers, managers having been able to devise responses which only offer to hold, monitor or police the client's behaviour with no permanent solution. Even so, this limited response reflects the statutory mandates that underlie much SSD work. So, when it comes to identifying areas which have some prospect of improving occupational power if the technology can be got right, work with children and their families holds out the most hope, or so it would appear, particularly for qualified workers attempting to develop and practise their professional skills.

It might therefore be expected that 'professional' techniques on the one hand and formal procedures and prescriptions as determined by managers on the other would be the two main response patterns. This appears to be the case according to the results described in Chapter 5. The balance, nevertheless, is tipped towards the managerially designed responses reflecting the current advantage that administrative technologies have in personal social services work. But the manager's viewpoint is not so strong as to preclude alternative worker perceptions of child care practice. Occasionally this may lead to conflict or resistance on the part of the worker. So it is then that cracks in 'managerial hegemony' are most likely to appear in child care work leading to the assertion of cruder but weaker forms of power: the use of hierarchical authority and coercion.

The trend, though, even in child care work, appears to be towards managers increasing their control over practice. Although large pockets of child care work have offered the prospect of occupational freedom, the lack of clear or demonstrable success has led to further restrictions placed around the worker's self-control. For example, recommendations which follow in the wake of enquiries into the death of children through non-accidental injury often suggest the need for tighter staff supervision and more coordination between different types and levels of worker. Monitoring and disciplining the worker's behaviour in order that she obey set procedures falls to managers to organise.

Thorpe's (Thorpe 1977, Thorpe 1979, Thorpe et al. 1979, Thorpe et al. 1980) recommendations arising out of his Intermediate Treatment studies also see an increase in management control. His work is particularly interesting because it records the effect of social workers increasing their licence to practise preventative and therapeutic skills in relation to adolescents who have offended and, more significantly, adolescents (and younger children) thought to be 'at risk' of offending. His investigations into the practice of IT and its effects demonstrate quite clearly that the results of social worker interventions of this kind have led to an increase in the number of young people placed on care orders, an increase in the number of children entering the orbit of SSDs and a consequential increase in costs to SSDs. It appears that professional efforts at preventing children coming into care has actually led to more children experiencing courts and care orders. Thorpe's prescription is that managers should impose tight criteria on the practices of IT workers, that they should curb professional autonomy and restrict the number and type of children receiving the specialist attention of 'professionals' in order to reduce the damage and harm being done.

SUMMARY

The ability of an occupational group to control the content of its own practice determines a range of phenomena. For social workers, these include the type of actions which take place in case practice and the organisation of fieldworkers and their work. The concept of control over the content of practice runs through and links each empirical level and its interpretation. The mechanism which helps explain the prevalence of standardised prescriptive 'service' responses in work with the elderly or the dissolution of professional discretion into administratively and statutorily determined procedure in work with children also explains the differential distribution of fieldworkers and client groups. Practice and organisation are understood as intimately linked phenomena.

Explanations of the behaviour of social workers in case practice tend to be approached solely in terms of 'professional' social work theories. If the social worker's practice is felt to be bureaucratically determined this is viewed as a matter of regret. Similarly, the prevailing organisation of social workers is judged in terms of the occupation's ability to establish its professional standing. The improved professional status of social workers is often taken as self-evidently desirable. Any limits placed on professional progress, that is increased worker control, is seen as bad. But the occupational limits and weaknesses are rarely taken as indicators of social work's actual nature and that its character can only be understood in a wider context which lies outside the control of social workers. In seeking to recognise common threads between the 'micro' and 'macro' levels of observation, not only is a close relationship argued between the details of practice and the organisation of fieldworkers but the nature of the activity itself is taken as embedded in its social context. As Salaman (1978, p.523) reminds his readers, 'organisations reflect and reveal societal resources and interests' and that 'the outside world is also inside', permeating the practices of the organisation and its workers.

10 The rise of the welfare manager

The scope for power and occupational control by social services managers and social workers has increased in the general expansion of the personal social services. Within this context social work is defined relative to the prevailing political fortunes and interests of the various occupations involved in the work. The discussion is developed through the following four stages:

1. The growth of the 'service classes'
2. The expansion of the personal social services
3. The weakness of social work's 'professional project'
4. The rise of the social services manager.

1. THE GROWTH OF THE 'SERVICE CLASSES'

The rise of professional, administrative and managerial employees, particularly in private and public bureaucracies, has represented something of a problem for social and class analysts. These occupational groups have been described as the 'service classes' by Renner (1953) and the Salaried Middle Class (SMC) by Gould (1980). Although such groups do not share the ownership of the means of production nor are they part of the elite of state power, their labour is nevertheless taken to be non-productive; 'they are not themselves a source of surplus value but, rather, a charge on the surplus value which is extracted ... from the working-class' (Goldthorpe 1982, p.167). The service classes occupy an 'intermediate stratum' between what Marxists have traditionally seen as a straight split between the classes representing capital and labour. More particularly, the growth in state activities and the increasing scale of technological and organisational pursuits has led to an expansion in the number of 'service class' employees. Goldthorpe (1982, p.172) estimates that they have risen from around 5-10% of the workforce at the beginning of the century to about 20-25% today.

Marxist writers have seen the service classes as essentially temporary. 'Members of these strata are destined to become assimilated either into the working class via a process of "proletarianisation" or conceivably, but to a lesser extent, into the capitalist class via a process of "incorporation"' (Goldthorpe 1982, p.162). A recent elaboration of this position is found in the work of Carchedi (1977). Johnson (1977) takes advantage of Carchedi's analysis to account for the professions in the class structure. Johnson explains that the middle classes can be identified with both capital and labour. Insofar as they are involved in the surveillance, control and maintenance of labour they are carrying out the functions of 'global capital'. But to the extent that people like managers, professionals and administrators are also involved in co-ordinating the labour process and providing specialist knowledge and expertise they are a necessary part of the production process; they are part of the 'collective labourer'.

The class position of professionals is both intermediate and ambiguous, but is likely to be resolved one way or the other. Professional work may become either (i) de-skilled, routinised and 'proletarianised', or (ii) identified and 'incorporated' with the owners of capital as they control the practices of productive workers. Johnson (1977, pp.106-107) cites accountancy as an example in which the 'profession' has been split in both these directions. A few high status accountants acting on behalf of capital actually design the routinised work practices and 'book-keeping' systems which are carried out by low level accountants. Their work is thereby pushed down to become a much closer part of the labour process. Thus, while top flight management based accountants serve capital and make their own work sufficiently 'indeterminate' not to be eligible for others to control, this 'very same function has the effect of stressing the technicality of the work activities of their colleague-subordinates, creating the conditions for work devaluation' (Johnson 1977, p.108).

Although Marxist analyses attempt to explain the professional success of different occupational groups by examining their

relation to capital and the labour process, there have been a
number of more recent attempts to understand the service
classes outside the simple dichotomy of capital and labour
(Goldthorpe 1982; Gould 1980). Marxist studies of the welfare
state see the provision of education, health and the social
services as benefiting capital (by the production of a healthy,
unassertive labour force leading to 'social harmony' (O'Connor
1973, p.6) and the conversion of the socially 'useless' into
productive individuals (Gouldner 1971, pp.76-77)). The political 'right' sees the working class as the main beneficiary of
the escalating costs of welfare (at the expense of investment
capital). Gould, however, suggests that the service classes or
the SMC are the prime beneficiaries of increased social
provision and state activity. Moreover, they act to consoli-
date and secure these benefits. Thus 'welfare bureaucracies
are run _by_ as well as _for_ the SMC' (Gould 1980, p.407). The
SMC have the ability to define needs and how they are to be
met. They have 'the ability to act in their own interests'
(Gould 1980, p.410). Like Johnson (1982), Gould sees the
emergence of the SMC and the modern state as closely linked
phenomena in which 'the corporate state is based on the values
and pursues the goals and interest of the SMC' (Gould 1980,
p.402).

Gould, in suggesting that 'control' is largely in the hands
of the SMC, provides the strongest argument for the existence
of an independent and self-interested service and middle class,
who benefit by the maintenance of the welfare state. The
notion is of a service class 'deploying strategies to preserve
and expand its own position' (Crompton and Jones 1984, p.223).
However, Crompton and Jones conclude their review of the
service classes by arguing that a distinct break between the
routine practices of the working class on the one hand and the
independent, discretionary practices of the service classes on
the other is too abrupt:

> Rather, there is a none-too-smooth continuum from routine
> ... to authoritative managerial work differentiated in
> functional terms and conditions of employment. We would
> argue, therefore, that rather than attempting to specify
> a 'service class', this situation is better understood as
> a continuum, with at one pole a group of 'de-skilled'
> routine workers, occupying 'proletarian' slots in the
> occupational structure, and at the other senior management
> level ... (Crompton and Jones 1984, p.224)

2. THE EXPANSION OF THE PERSONAL SOCIAL SERVICES

According to Ham and Hill (1984, p.23), the state can be defined in terms of the institutions which make it up and the

functions these institutions perform. One of the main roles of the state is the maintenance of law and order. More recently it has become heavily involved in the provision of services and in the operation of the economy. Indeed what appears 'distinctive about the modern state is the character and scope of its intervention' (Ham and Hill 1984, p.22).

The state's growing involvement in the population's welfare and behaviour throughout the twentieth century has led to a considerable expansion in social services including the personal social services. Abercrombie and Urry (1983, p.4) write that social welfare workers increased some twenty fold between 1911 and 1981. During the 1970s the proportion of all public expenditure devoted to the personal social services doubled, rising from 0.9 to 1.9 per cent (Goldberg and Hatch 1981, p.1), representing the biggest increase of local authority expenditure by any service. Renner, in introducing the notion of the service classes, placed social services personnel ('the distributive agents of welfare') within this class (see Goldthorpe 1982, p.167). Indeed, some observers of the Seebohm reorganisations of SSDs see the expansion benefiting mainly welfare managers and social work professionals and no one else (Gough 1979, p.94; Leonard 1974).

Certainly, the amalgamation and expansion of the personal social services produced a much bigger pool for welfare personnel. Between 1971 and 1974 the number of social workers increased by over 50% (Bamford 1982, p.5). But not all were destined to grow in size and occupational stature. Within the new SSDs there was a greater range of opportunities, responsibilities and power available which could either be spread uniformly across different occupational groups in structurally flat organisations or stratified within pyramidal structures with some groups achieving a lot of control leaving others with little. Securing control over the content of work obliged different groups to establish the relevance of their skills to the expectations contained in the legislation and the resources provided to back the existence of state welfare agencies. Whether control would be spread evenly or concentrated in the hands of a few would, in turn, have a direct bearing on the type of organisational structure adopted.

Thus, expansion of the personal social services might not lead to a simple growth of all the service class occupations. Rather, there might be the opportunity for some groups to increase their control at the expense of others whose work, as a consequence, might become more routine, programmed and directed - in short 'proletarianised'. The occupational fortunes of the various types of fieldworker have to be understood as part of the process in which politicians, managers and practitioners compete to control both the way the work is understood and the responses made in the light of that understanding.

3. THE WEAKNESS OF THE 'PROFESSIONAL PROJECT' OF FIELD SOCIAL WORKERS

The state's support of the personal social services creates two areas over which occupations might seek responsibility and control: (i) the administration and organisation of the state's delegated authority to respond to social problems and needs, and (ii) the specialist knowledge and skills to tackle effectively the social problems and needs as defined by the state.

To some extent, the strategies used by managers and professionals remain in opposition. In order for managers to have things understood their way, professionals have to relinquish some of their control and vice versa. Managerial strategies are designed to minimise reliance on the skills of other groups leading to increased control over the organisation's goals and values. As we have seen, the strategies used include the breaking down and routinisation of specialised and complex actions (through a process of de-skilling). In this way those who previously had special and valuable talents lose their claim to privileged treatment. Similarly, those who believe that they have important knowledge and specialised practical skills will seek to resist managerial control and the implied downgrading of their work.

> Professionalism entails an alternative form of the division of labour which replaces bureaucratic authority ... Where occupational authority is dominant, the <u>work task</u>, 'who is to perform it and the way it is performed and evaluated is controlled by the men who actually perform productive labour' ... Thus, authority is predicated on institutionalised expertise ... In medicine, for example, the division of labour is ordered and coordinated by a dominant profession rather than by management. (Johnson 1977, p.97)

Two basic areas of work remain outside the control of present day field social workers: (i) the determination of clients and their needs (the 'problem') and (ii) the character of the responses available (the method). Both of these are defined by the state. So for example, 'the client of the probation officer', writes Johnson (1977, p.108), 'is ... <u>produced</u> and guaranteed by the workings of the system of justice'. This style of analysis has been picked up or echoed by only a few writers about social work. Their argument has been that, sociologically, social workers have a necessary and integral relationship with the state and society; it is in the nature of the occupation as currently defined (Davies, M. 1981; Howe 1979; Philp 1979). Whereas managers tend to accept this state of affairs and attune their skills accordingly, practitioners have been less reliable, particularly in accepting the broad character of statutorily ordained responses. Occupational groups that hint at understanding things differently without guaranteeing the outcome of their efforts are unlikely to receive much in the way of delegated authority and discretion. This is the case with social workers. And it is managers who have picked up the task of restricting, controlling and organising social workers and their responses. This has further enhanced the occupational power of managers (e.g. see Parry, Rustin and Satyamurti (eds) 1979 passim).

For social workers, the growth in state activity in the personal social services has done two things. It has promoted the scale and scope of the occupation's interests. But the state's very ability to define and create the work of the personal social services denies the occupation itself control over the content of its own practice. In advancing the intimate relationship between the state and the professions, Johnson clearly rebuts the idea that the professions contain any transcendent qualities said to lie in their knowledge and skill base.

> The alternative history of the state/profession relationship, which stresses the autonomy of the professions, retains a view of the state as interventionist and repressive but seeks the source of occupational autonomy in some _essence_ of professionalism which lies beyond the power of the state to control - variously characterised as competence, expertise, knowledge, technique, etc. Thus, the complexity of occupational knowledge and the esoteric nature of occupational expertise or technique is seen as the mirror of this alternative history realised as a process of professionalisation ... A common version of the autonomy thesis is where occupational technique is viewed as operating as a universal limitation on state power. Technique stands outside of and determines the outcome of power relations. According to such a thesis the autonomy of an occupation is secured so long as the occupation is free from 'technical evaluation' by the state. However, what goes to make up professional practice, including technique, may itself be an outcome of the state/profession relationship. (Johnson 1982, pp.189-90)

Social workers have been accused of failing to deliver the goods. Their style of practice and choice of intellectual support has meant that at the very least it has been easy to dismiss social workers as professional lightweights. A number of reasons contribute to the weakness of social work's 'professional project', some of which amount to them being hoisted by their own petard. Such reasons can be gathered under two main headings: technological and ideological.

Firstly, there are the technological weaknesses (e.g. Fischer 1973; Reid and Hanrahan 1981). There has been a long established habit in social work, particularly during training, to hitch the professional star to science. Social workers have regularly and repeatedly chosen to see themselves as applied behavioural and social scientists. Following the adoption of a scientific stance is the implicit and often explicit aim of cure, with the suggestion that the practitioner can predict and control the outcome. There is no professional mileage to be gained, therefore, by wasting therapeutic skills in trying to redeem the irredeemable, hence the relative absence of qualified workers in work with the elderly and handicapped. Social workers continue to understand themselves as curers of the socially and behaviourally incurable. And it is on this self-inflicted claim that they are often judged. Delinquents do not appear to stop being delinquents and neglectful parents continue to neglect their children in spite of the efforts of social workers.

Social work behaviour in critical and sensitive areas (except in legal terms or very specific or trivial instances where, for example, behavioural techniques might succeed) no more guarantees a particular outcome than the efforts of many other concerned people. Social work either has not got the technology, or more likely, it is not that sort of business. In Mattinson and Sinclair's work, the authors observed that in order to reduce demands to manageable proportions, social workers were 'left with clients who for reasons of public concern, statutory requirements and common humanity were considered high priority or were demanding. They were not, however, the most amenable to treatment.' (1979, pp.294-95). In his study of an SSD team, Corby (1982, p.634) records that 'social work with long term clients was not characterised by problem solving activity'. The agency did not appear to lend itself to this type of work and 'so there was little emphasis on strategy or the means of achieving goals' (p.634). Although assessments might have been 'professionally informed', actual intervention seemed agency-determined, suggesting a split between professional theory and departmental practice with the latter in the ascendant.

It would seem, therefore, that for many conventionally trained social workers, life in large social work departments is frustrating; they sense that their professional talents are either irrelevant, inappropriate or ineffective. The power of workers is related to the degree to which they are able to minimise uncertainty for the organisation. If the occupation's technology does not reduce uncertainty, that occupation will remain relatively weak.

Secondly, there are the <u>ideological</u> 'weaknesses'. Rather than convert clients into technical problems, the ideological stance prefers to see them as moral and political questions (Esland 1976, p.56). Although seeing the client's point of view is a feature, indeed a principle of social work practice, it can sometimes be criticised as showing softness, gullibility or inappropriate tolerance. This is a principle that does not encourage others to view the social worker as someone whose judgement can be trusted or whose practice has credibility. Others can doubt the wisdom of social workers 'siding' with their clients. It hints at their professional dubiety, that they might not entirely be playing the game. If social workers are people who are inclined to sympathise with clients, their occupational freedom to make 'on-the-job' responses and their wish to see their clients their way will be questioned, particularly as clients have been defined by society. Such judgements are unlikely to promote the achievement of occupational self-control. As Pearson (1973) sees it, social workers can be viewed as 'social bandits', conducting scurries on the margins of society, robbing the rich to give to the poor, a 'privatised solution to public ills'. Social work has been said to deal in 'precarious values' (Clark 1956) about which the public remains profoundly ambivalent. It is the case that 'social workers are rarely free to choose whatever ideology they please, because their practices are ... bounded by systems over which they have little control' (Hardiker 1981, p.100).

Perhaps the cardinal sin for a social worker is not only to take the client's side, but to go further and blame the state for people's troubles. If this is how social workers see their role when they presume to define how things are, then they are certainly not going to be given a chance to control their own activities. Occupations spawned and sponsored by the state cannot expect to prosper if they bite the hand that feeds them. To repeat, 'the ideological bases of indetermination are not available for the purposes of occupational exploitation' (Johnson 1977, p.108). Or as Perrow (1972, p.151) cynically puts it 'the important point for organisational theory is that it is on the basis of the regulatory functions that organisations are judged, not their announced service goals. Wardens are not fired for not rehabilitating prisoners; psychiatric administrators or therapists for not curing the insane; welfare administrators for not getting people to work or mending broken homes ... But failure to control, buy off, or segregate his or her charges will bring trouble.'

The timing of the negative research studies into the effectiveness of social work practice (e.g. Fisher 1973; Mullen and Dumpson 1973) and the radical critique of mainstream social work in the early 1970s could hardly have been worse for an occupation whose respect and status were in need of confirmation. Traditional casework practice was being undermined on two of its major foundations: its technology and its ideology. But insofar as remedies were proffered by these critics they failed to relate in any acceptable way to the needs and expectations of personal social services practice. The behavioural formulae of scientific caseworkers and the revolutionary rhetoric of radicals spoke little that was understood by state welfare workers. Their messages were seen as irrelevant to the task in hand (Cohen 1975). Both failed social work.

The vacuum left between them was filled by the role of organisational manager. The manager employed a very different kind of competence and one that did not ignore the rules of the game. The growing scale of welfare work and the alleged misperformances of social workers provided a clear opportunity for managers with their methods based on an ability to simplify, coordinate, standardise, regularise and check the efforts of workers in the field. So long as social workers insist on defining themselves as either traditional change agents (the therapeutic approach) backed by a weak technology or as arbiters of political and ideological truths (the radical approach), their occupational ambitions will remain frustrated. Or as Butrym (1976, p.12) puts it, 'inherent in the nature of social work is its vulnerability to distortion either in the direction of psychotherapy or politics'. The practitioner in the welfare professions 'can never forget that he is a living embodiment of public sentiments and that these must not be outraged' (Nokes, 1967, p.32).

Lipsky's (1980) notion of the 'street level bureaucrat' encapsulates some of the forlorn hopes - both technical and ideological - of welfare workers. People often enter public employment 'with at least some commitment to service. Yet the very nature of this work prevents them from coming close to the ideal conception of their jobs ... huge caseloads and inadequate resources combine with the uncertainties of method and the unpredictability of clients to defeat their aspirations as service workers' (p. xii). There is a feeling of not being in control of either outcomes or the 'raw materials' (client's circumstances). So, although social work professionals appear to have considerable pockets of freedom and discretion, the anxieties and uncertainties of the work lead them to adopt routinised, limited and rule-bound practices (Smith 1981). Indeed, Smith (1981, p.49) in his studies, came to believe that 'the behaviour of the professional social workers was ...

rather predictable'.

4. THE RISE OF THE SOCIAL SERVICES MANAGER AND BUREAUCRATIC CONTROL

The weakness of the 'professional project' of social workers, their inability to develop a technology that is either demonstrably effective or relevant to much of the work as defined, means that the broad control and organisation of the personal social services is available to managers. 'Where the professional element is weak', writes Mishra (1981, p.129), 'the services may have a greater tendency towards bureaucratisation'. And in times of change and uncertainty, 'Any group with a clear idea of how to proceed must be well placed to gain a strong position', which is exactly what welfare managers have done according to Glastonbury et al. (1980, p.40).

Even though most managers are professionally qualified social workers, their skills and interests have shifted and been encouraged towards management based technologies and ideas. Indeed, across all the health and welfare services throughout the 1970s there was an emphasis on establishing managerial control and achieving administrative rationality using ideas derived from business management (Cawson 1982, p.84; Kakabadse 1982, pp.42 and 51). In particular, the Seebohm Report and the early designs for the shape of SSDs received much inspiration from models of industrial design (Glastonbury et al. 1980, p.45; Leonard 1978, p.47). This allowed the rise of the welfare manager. 'It is not surprising', note Glastonbury et al. (1980, p.71), '... to find management developing a wide range of control procedures, both for their own security, and to cope with the ongoing instability of the front line'. Managers and bureaucratic organisation therefore arose out of a particular context in which other occupations and their techniques failed to have a convincing or acceptable impact on the job as perceived by those who couched the legislation, provided the resources or sanctioned the responses. In this sense, social workers have got the organisation they deserve. And so Bamford (1982), himself a manager, is able to write that the aim of his book on managing social work is 'to develop the argument that skilled and sensitive management can have an immense influence on the quality of current practice' (p.1) and ends by saying that social work autonomy and decision-making ability is necessarily limited by agency expectations, political constraints and resource availability (pp.171-72). 'It is important', Bamford concludes, 'that a strong planning and policy-making capacity should be retained centrally' (p.186).

The rise of the welfare manager has a number of implications and consequences for social workers, their practice and organisation. These implications are pursued in the following sequence:

- (i) The manager's definition of social services and social work
- (ii) Types of worker and their training
- (iii) Form of organisation
- (iv) The views and experiences of social workers in SSDs
- (v) Forms of occupational organisation for social workers: unionisation.

(i) The manager's definition of social services and social work

Managers define the 'task environment' in such a way that it accords with the political and legislative outlook of the agency whilst at the same time suiting their own technical skills and understandings. For example, by redefining work as straightforward, lacking any significant uncertainty which might tax the rehabilitative resources of the organisation, the only control potential left in such work accrues to those who make the decisions to prescribe and downgrade the work in the first place. This is the fate of services offered to the elderly and disabled. Managers value a stable, orderly relationship with their environment. The drive towards reducing uncertainty often takes the form of standardising transactions to make the work more uniform and therefore more manageable. So, GPs medical certificates have to be written before telephones can be provided. Case conferences have to be convened when non-accidental injury is suspected. Managers, therefore, are people who do a number of key things:

- (a) They define the parameters of practice; they develop the systems, procedures and tasks which help tackle matters rationally.
- (b) They coordinate and unify the workers and their work which they have programmed and divided.
- (c) They introduce 'form' and 'shape' to the disparate efforts of basic grade workers.
- (d) They control resources (e.g. the number of home help hours).
- (e) They devise the normative structure of the organisation.

These activities are the very stuff of control. Managers extract whatever uncertainty there is in the process so that their 'act' of devising the systems of practice, surveillance and resource allocation which determines the work of subordinates remains the major free act in the whole business. The 'language of rational policy-making, being the mode of discourse of the large firm' (Cawson 1982, p.84), was used by social services managers to curb the power of 'professionals'. Policies are a means of exercising control. Managerialism is part of the post-war emphasis in social services on rational processes of management. In this way the Seebohm Report (p.184) believed that 'The effective exercise of delegated authority necessarily implies that the headquarters should produce statements of guidance on general policy'. Procedures, manuals and checks tie practice to the logic of management. Work design is a strategy of control. Less is required of the worker; less responsibility, less initiative, less discretion, less imagination. And in return less is given; less control, less power, less money.

(ii) Types of worker and their training

Perrow (1965, pp.947-48) argues that 'changing conceptions of the nature of the human material' leads 'to different conceptions of the tasks that should be performed on or for them'. With significant areas of social services and social work seen as straightforward and capable of being handled by a combination of task routinisation, prescription and resource availability, there is less need for the fieldwork force to be entirely staffed by 'professionally' orientated practitioners.

Satyamurti (1981, p.185) notes that the widespread feeling that the old casework skills had been lost upon reorganisation, combined with an increase in organisational size, led radicals to refer to their departments as 'Seebohm factories', 'with its connotations of a shift from craft work to assembly line manufacture'. As students emerge from training with a basic professional qualification, a Social Work Today editorial (1.8.78) observed that 'they enter departments where they are systematically deskilled and depersonalised'. Casework was often seen as irrelevant and inappropriate. 'Yet there was no new skill to take its place, no new technique or systematic body of knowledge. Social workers spent a considerable amount of time on routine tasks and administrative work involving little or no skill' (Satyamurti 1981, p.185). And with these changes in the design of practice we observe not only the apparent deskilling of the professional worker but also the increasing use of the 'unskilled' labourer - the social work assistant in the social services departments and the ancillary in the probation service.

Managerialism has proved to be pervasive and seems to have reversed many of the hopes of the early supporters of the Seebohm Report. The expectation was that after reorganisation, the welfare tradition offering routine agency services would succumb to the sophisticated skills of the independent and individualised practices of professionals. In the event, many would claim that the <u>reverse</u> has happened: that now, not only is work with the old and handicapped still handled bureaucratically, but much child care, mental health and family work is prone increasingly to management predetermination. Hey (1982, p.17) describes SSDs as 'bigger and better welfare departments'. Put another way, the worker now preferred by many senior managers is more likely to have the characteristics of the old, untrained welfare worker than the newly trained holder of the CQSW.

Many directors of social services would like to see training more closely linked with their own departments so that a more amenable, more compatible sort of fieldworker is produced. Mary Hope (1977, p.26), an SSD training officer, has written that 'regarding the appropriateness of the training job, it is almost universally acknowledged that the CQSW prepares students for a task that it is not possible to do within the current local authority Social Services Department organisation'. Shaw and Walton (1978) believed that 'Directors are ever tempted to demand neatly packaged social workers, trained to follow agency rules without question'. And a group of 15 heads of CQSW courses said that what departments wanted was 'compliant technicians' who would uncomplainingly implement agency procedures (Akhurst 1980). Kakabadse (1982) confirms these fears. From his studies of fieldworkers it appears that 'the message offered a social worker on leaving the organisation to meet his client, is to remain within the rules and regulations already established' (Kakabadse 1982, p.112) or as one worker put it 'I have learnt that we are local government officers first and a social worker second ... nobody can act outside the law and nobody can act outside their policy' (p.114).

Of course, there now exists a model for training workers in the management mould. The Certificate of Social Service (CSS) is a more modest qualification than the CQSW based on in-service training and day release. It was originally designed for social work assistants, home help organisers, residential workers - people who often work in a prescribed fashion with second class client groups like the old and disabled. If the activities of social workers are to be more circumscribed and subject to control, then it follows that a CSS type training would make managerial sense.

Whereas training is an appropriate experience for those carrying out prescribed tasks, professional education suggests that practitioners, acting autonomously, should also be able to enquire and understand the 'reason why' of things. CSS courses <u>train</u> people. 'Training suggests the acquisition of appropriate appraisals and habits of response in limited conventional situations; it lacks the wider cognitive implications of "education"'

(Peters 1966, p.33). Given the present views of welfare work
by many social services managers, a suitable fieldworker is
more likely to be the product of training and not education.
As two directors of SSDs put it, at least the CSS trains people
'to do the job asked of them' (quoted in Jones 1983, p.118).

The CCETSW (1983) working group's review, Qualifying Teaching
Policies Paper 20:1, attempts to take training matters a stage
further. It suggests the scrapping of the CSS and the CQSW and
replacing them with one basic qualification for all fieldworkers and residential workers. The proposed new qualification, with its appeal to SSD managers, is more like the basic
training concept entailed in the CSS. 'The distinction between
social work and social services', report the working group,
'which has been relevant in the past now seems to us inappropriate' (p.3). Although the Council accepts that there is a
need to respect the independence of educational institutions,
it nevertheless suggests that 'proposals for education and
training programmes submitted to the Council for approval are
endorsed by both employer and professional interests, and are
not simply devised and presented by educational institutions'
(p.7). And in similar mood the Standing Conference Certificate
in Social Service (1983) proposes a model for integrating
training in the personal social services. 'Training should be
based on an analysis of tasks, skills and knowledge required to
meet service objectives' (p.1) and training ought to be more
related to work requirements with students being selected by
agencies as well as colleges (pp.6 and 2).

(iii) Form of organisation

The style of organisation 'determines the kind of policies
which can be effectively implemented' (Webb and Wistow 1982,
p.20). 'Mechanistic' forms of organisation suit managerially
based control strategies. Black et al. (1983, p.201) observed
that central management in SSDs determined the structure and
that in 'Aber', for example, 'this reflected senior management's desire to impose county-wide uniformity' on area teams.
Various combinations of centralisation and formalisation within
pyramidal and hierarchical authority structures become the
prevailing pattern of organisation for most SSDs. With this
type of structure managers are able to (i) determine tasks and
resource distribution, and (ii) coordinate the order and
relationships between these two and those who carry out the
work. Managers 'create, co-ordinate and control' the division
of labour (Johnson 1977, p.97).

Increasingly, social workers find themselves in a world of
the manager's manufacture: caseload management techniques,
priority scaling, review forms, practice manuals, procedure

charts. In carrying out such tasks, not only is the social worker more effectively managed, but her 'skill is redefined to incorporate the management skill of manpower control' (Lee 1982, p.29).

According to Glastonbury et al. (1980, p.71) one county SSD had over 400 different forms and several hundred pages of detailed administrative instructions. Jones (1983, pp.123-24) mentions Gateshead SSD having 96 different forms to be used by social workers as the department seeks 'to regulate the activities of social workers in their direct contact with clients'. As social workers become more like peripatetic clerks, with forms and check lists governing the content of practice between worker and client, the worker has less and less room for manoeuvre. In the wake of tighter procedures, more categoric review forms and priority scalings, the use of computers and the associated ticking of more boxes appears increasingly common in SSDs. In Gateshead, for example, Jones (1983, pp.127-130) notes that computerisation was said to improve labour management, offering greater control over what social workers do and bringing 'much needed discipline to case recording'. In these administratively saturated climates, workers felt they had little independence; case review systems are imposed, supervisory checks increased and workers are 'constantly reminded about their overriding responsibility to the agency' (Black et al. 1983, pp.204-208). And in more specialised areas too, case control is shifted more to the centre. Shearer (in Glastonbury et al. 1980, p.80) describes the use in one SSD of 'two formidable large red books' of rules and guidelines to be used in child care cases which must be followed to the letter. Generally, the main response of SSDs to the problem of non-accidental injury to children has been an administrative one in which procedures act as administrative controls over social work practice (Glastonbury et al. 1980, Chapter 7).

In his research, Kakabadse (1982, p.7) hypothesised that the Seebohm proposals led to a rise in bureaucracy in SSDs, this in spite of the many early recommendations that welfare organisations should avoid mechanistic designs and go for some flexible, organic form of structure (e.g. Algie 1970; Barter 1969). However, simply to recommend a form of organisation misses the point that a particular organisational structure represents a kind of control by a particular occupational group. Different groups assert different types of control over their work and hence require different types of organisation. Control based on specialist knowledge and skills leading to structures favouring professional groups cannot be simply recommended as preferable. Kakabadse (1982, pp.64-65) sees the amount of routine work in SSDs to be a good indicator of the degree of job regulation and rule observation present. SSD workers appear to see their departments 'as centralised in terms of decision making' with 'daily work ... restricted by rule and procedure leading to a feeling of routineness'. Supervisors were thought to be heavily involved in decisions taken. In general, 'respondents indicate that the way the organisations are established has little to do with their professional training and professional interests' (Kakabadse 1982, p.67). 'For social workers', notes Satyamurti (1981, p.23), '... statutory duties were the framework within which their objectives were formulated; for the Director, they constituted the objectives themselves'. Crompton and Jones (1984, p.226) identify what they believe is a long run tendency for managers to centralise control 'not just of the labour force, but also of investment, policy, decisions', so that it becomes more focussed rather than diffused.

(iv) The views and experiences of social workers in SSDs

Most fieldworkers are reported as describing SSDs as bureaucratic. There is a general feeling of being over managed and that practice is constrained (Jones 1983, Chapter 7; Satyamurti 1981; Stevenson and Parsloe 1978, p.315), with fieldworkers feeling that they are only cogs in the great departmental machine. Cawson (1982, p.97) believes that 'managerialism ... has probably gone further in social work than in any other area of social policy'. In Black et al's (1983, p.202) study of SSDs, they repeatedly observe that workers felt rule bound and centrally directed, that 'social workers were not masters of their own destiny' which resulted in feelings of 'powerlessness', 'frustration and resentment' (p.215).

The respondents in Kakabadse's study saw their SSD as formalised. Fieldworkers saw themselves 'not in control of their job content' (1982, p.64), restricted and lacking 'information about projects and other programmes in the organisation' which serve to generate feelings of animosity towards management (p.107). Fieldworkers who feel that they have little power to influence management or effect change become 'free to blame management for the undesirable features of their own situation' (Mattinson and Sinclair 1979, p.279). The prevalence of such negative views indicates that there is at least a verbal resistance by fieldworkers to management control strategies. This absence of ideological control requires managers to use less subtle forms of power including pulling rank, and the establishment of a less skilled, more compliant workforce.

(v) Forms of occupational organisation for social workers: unionisation

The construction of social work organisations along business management lines coupled with the fieldworker's perceptual shift from independent professional to local government employee has encouraged many basic grade workers to associate in trade unions rather than professional organisations. The role and power of trade unions has been an increasingly important dimension in the working conditions and practices of many SSD employees (Parry and Parry 1979, pp.43-44).

It seems no accident that the first major strikes in social work came in the late 1970s when the initial dust had settled on SSDs and their real shape had become clear. Organising along professional lines suggests that the workers see themselves as having achieved some control over their own practice. Turning to trade unionism indicates that fieldworker interests are no longer synonymous with those of their employer. Jones (1983, Chapter 7) in his review of social workers as potentially 'difficult employees', concludes that employers and managers believe that professional workers 'should be unquestioningly loyal to the council's policies'. In devising organisations and procedures to ensure employee conformity, professional autonomy is undermined and trade unionism appears to be a more appropriate form of worker organisation (Jones 1983, Chapter 8).

11 Occupational control and the nature of social work

The current state of social work practice and organisation in SSDs is rarely viewed with satisfaction. There appear to be three types of observer. Each diagnoses the ills of social work from a particular perspective and then proceeds to offer prescriptions. The first sees social work as technologically weak. Proposals are made to strengthen the knowledge base and technical skills of the profession. The second sees social work as inappropriately organised. Remedies usually include giving the worker more freedom in organisations which are decentralised. There exists a third view which is less commonly heard. This looks at the personal social services and their organisation from outside the egocentrism of the social work profession. It prefers to understand the occupation and its practice in relation to other factors including the social, political and value climate in which social work has its being.

TECHNICAL DIAGNOSES AND PRESCRIPTIONS

A wide literature exists which regards the performance of social workers as either technologically weak or ideologically suspect. The beleaguered state of social work is explained in terms of these weaknesses. If social workers were to strengthen their technological base or alter their ideological outlook, so the arguments go, the occupation either would command greater occupational credibility (for example, for it to become more scientific: Brewer and Lait 1980; Sheldon 1978) or would acquire greater moral integrity (for example, for it to become more politically relevant: Corrigan and Leonard 1978; Simpkin 1979).

Like so many 'panaceas' for social work practice, each technological fashion requires the world to be bent to fit its shape. This privilege is rarely accorded social workers as the benefits remain either unproven, unconvincing or inappropriate to the work in hand. The danger is that in fitting the world to the technique, social work itself becomes distorted. The technician though, feels that she is being - wilfully - confined by agencies who effectively clip her professional wings. Managers become sceptical about the need for specialist techniques in many day-to-day practices and see 'social work' as too refined and precious a thing for the rough and busy life of over-stretched SSDs.

But the basic point remains. The general use of a particular technology cannot be established prior to a group achieving occupational strength. Only with strength does the occupation have the ability to define the world in such a way that its technologies are seen as appropriate. Control precedes technological imperialism and control has to be achieved. Technological prescriptions as the remedy for social work's weak condition fail to recognise that techniques are not ends. To ignore the ends of social work that currently hold sway in SSDs is to seriously question the relevance of many social work theories and techniques.

ORGANISATIONAL DIAGNOSES AND PRESCRIPTIONS

Over the years, on both sides of the Atlantic, the organisation has been blamed for the difficulties experienced by professional social workers (e.g. Farmer et al. 1977; Finch 1976). Instead of bureaucratically and managerially controlled forms of practice and organisation, the prescription usually entails some form of decentralisation of authority and control away from managers and to field social workers. This line of thinking extends right up to the present with arguments for patch-based practice and neighbourhood teams (Hadley and McGrath 1981). Pinker (1984) pejoratively describes this prescription as a form of 'populism', part of the disenchantment with the complexity of modern industrial life.

But again, asking for more control and power is one thing, being given it is another. The argument has been that the organisation itself represents a method of control and that control itself is an accomplishment. Groups in control arrange things to suit their concerns. Shifts in control not only represent changes in how the world is to be seen but also imply that things would be better viewed in this way - though better for whom remains the critical question.

THE ORGANISATION OF WORKERS AND THE CONTENT OF PRACTICE

In describing and explaining the distribution and differentiation of social workers and their practice, an attempt has been made to understand the work in terms of the ability of different occupational groups to control what the work means. Social work is an activity determined relative to the political and technical fortunes of the various groups competing to control an area of work. Social work has no essential nature. Its existence, its characteristics and style are a product of time, place and the balance of power between those occupations interested in tackling certain types of behaviour and social concerns.

'Professional' organisations have no special insight into the work or god-given right to reveal the 'real' nature of social work. Their definitions reflect and suit their interests. By the same token it remains the case that any occupational group can argue its views on how things should be understood. Although they remain weak under present circumstances, it could be that shifts in the political outlook or changes in the technical base of professional practitioners could alter the current climate in which social work is understood.

An existential view of social work has been offered, an activity whose nature is determined by its circumstances. Such a view not only accounts for prevailing definitions of the work but also determines the kinds of worker best suited to carry them out. Understanding the work and the worker in a particulaw way determines the form of organisational structure adopted. Organisational structure reflects whether control over the content of practice lies with either workers or managers. In this way, the organisation of social workers in SSDs reveals something of what social work means in the context of the personal social services.

Analysts in this mould are either realists or pessimists. Pinker (a realist) believes that the present model of client-centred social work is basically sound, 'but in need of a better defined and less ambitious mandate' (Pinker 1982, p.237). 'Social work should be explicitly selective rather than universalist in focus, reactive rather than preventive in approach' (p.237). Pinker goes on:

It is more practical to define the role and tasks of social work in terms of the range of activities which social workers undertake in response to certain institutional imperatives. The first set of imperatives derives from the range and variety of needs that confront social workers. The second is contained in the legislation that defines their mandatory local authority obligations and also indicates the range of their permissive undertakings. The third relates to the employers - statutory or otherwise - to whom social workers are accountable, who are themselves accountable in the discharge of their mandatory and permissive undertakings. (Pinker 1982, p.237)

(Thus) The first duty of a social worker is to do his job within the terms of reference presented by his local authority, and he is solely accountable to his local authority in a legal and contractual sense. (Pinker 1982, p.244)

More pessimistically, Black et al. (1983) conclude that because social work is bound to the state and its legal strictures impregnated as they are with issues of accountability, any attempts to shift practice in the direction of worker control or community based practice look most unpromising. This being the case, change in practice is only possible through alterations in the legal and administrative structures and this, they feel, is unlikely to happen (p.225). The authors speculate that the Barclay Report, like the Seebohm Report before it, will fail in its hopes because it fails to recognise the intimate relationship that exists between social workers, and the statutory origins of clients and the state (p.241). So, 'any attempt to divorce practice from the administrative determinants of effective service delivery would be like taking a scalpel away from a surgeon' (p.216).

SSD managers interpret welfare legislation, determine the resources to meet legal needs, design the systems which allow statutory matters to be handled. In doing this they accept the political parameters of social services and social work practice. Again Pinker (1982) recognises this when he says that 'To a very large extent the expectations that employers have of their social workers are directly determined by legislative imperatives. The autonomy of the employing bodies derives from the freedom with which they can organise their own social services ...' (p.251). Managers take a fairly literal reading of the legislation and so understand the elderly, for example, as making particular, specific and regular demands of the organisation for which relatively unskilled workers are perfectly appropriate.

NEW OUTLOOKS AND THE NATURE OF PRACTICE

Given the present predilections of professional social workers, the views of managers and their organisation of welfare might seem a not unreasonable attempt to deliver the personal social services. However, given their role as managers (and not practitioners) they are necessarily at a distance from the action. This remains a basic weakness. As Mant (1979, p.119) puts it in his book on British managers, 'the more removed you are from consumers on the one hand and those who actually make the products on the other, the more likely it is that the process of management may seem to have nothing to do with either'. At the moment, then, it may be thought that personal social services work suffers the worst of both worlds: weak, ineffectual fieldwork and strong but remote managers. And yet out of these observations a new arrangement of practice and its organisation might be discerned.

First, the prospect relies on social workers accepting that they do not have a special expertise in human relationships. 'The possibility of a science of human relationships with the certainty of the natural sciences does not exist, and hence that there is serious doubt about the reality of a social work expertise based exclusively on it' (Downie and Loudfoot 1978, p.119). Many social work skills appear to be the normal skills of sociable living (Pinker 1982, p.237). Downie and Loudfoot (1978, p.122) summarise the argument as follows:

> No amount of knowledge of what is the case can ever establish for us what we ought to do about it. The need for practical judgement of what we ought to do, granted our knowledge, is inescapable; and therefore there are radical limits to the possibility of expertise ... It is on the connection between his own everyday problems and those of his client, rather than on any doubtful connection between the natural and social sciences, that social work education should concentrate.

Second, the view rests on a new interpretation of the old social work adage 'start where the client is'. If the client and his statutory characteristics are defined by the law and the community, this is where the social worker starts. This remains true whether the social worker's responsibilities are spelt out under mandatory or permissive legislation. She has to accept this critical nature of the relationship between the client and the state and her own position within it.

The third element is really an extension of the second. Knowledge and practical judgement are accomplished when the practitioner does not have the broad canvas of life before her but chooses to concentrate on certain details of it. Specialisation - not so much of method - in client group or setting brings knowledge and expertise of a different kind to those based on the application of social and behavioural skills. Specialisation is already accepted as a desirable condition for the worker in the field of mental illness with the need for workers to be officially approved. It seems likely that similar demands will soon be made in respect of other vulnerable client groups. Pinker (1982, p.249) predicts children as next in line to warrant specialist workers. This would leave only the old and handicapped, fields in which once again workers might end up specialising by default.

So, rather than fight SSDs, the state and management, social workers are likely to gain in strength by recognising the name of the game, the basic preconditions that surround their work. In different ways the work of Hazel (1981) fostering difficult adolescents and Challis and Davies (1980) keeping old people out of residential care illustrate the themes of this section. The workers in both projects did not presume to be experts in human relationships. Neither therapy nor the direct giving of care were seen as the prerogative of social workers. Rather, in Hazel's work, 'expertise in human relationships and child rearing' is 'possessed by ordinary people leading successful family lives in the community' (Hazel 1982, p.20). In the work of Challis and Davies the caring skills of neighbours, members of the local community and other professions, are tapped in order to support old people in their own homes. The workers were also specialists. And whereas bureaucratic procedures may attempt to 'fix' clients and lock them into the grid of services and responses which exist already, the project workers attempted to design services and responses around the needs of the client. Workers became assessors, managers, coordinators; in short 'practitioner-managers' (Howe 1983).

Explicit in each project was that the worker be given a greater control over her work - over budgets, resources and decisions. Such decentralisation of control was not granted unquestioningly. As Challis and Davies record, some time had to be spent convincing the SSD committee that the project workers should have increased powers and autonomy. If such resistance was met in time-limited demonstration projects staffed by high quality workers, the prospects for large scale shifts in control do not look promising. The assumption of political and administrative control by workers conflicts with the interests and self-perceived skills of politicians and managers alike. Nevertheless, social workers have little choice but to accept the defining boundaries of their practice. It is no good their jeering from the sidelines. As an occupational group, social workers have to join in; they have to explore and understand the nature of their work from within its current confines rather than come along with a new set of rules and expect everyone else to stop playing the old game and try the new one.

These prescriptions demand patience as well as a willingness to renounce the narcissistic and immodest proclivities implied in many of social work's theoretical interests. If the organisation of fieldworkers and their practice in SSDs reveals the relative nature of social work and the present limits of social workers' occupational power and if social workers are encouraged to embrace this understanding, the occupationally meek may find that they inherit more of the world of the personal social services than if they remain ambitious and grand-minded.

Bibliography

Abercrombie, Nicholas and Urry, John, (1983), Capital, Labour and the Middle Classes, George Allen and Unwin, London.
Addison, Carole, (1982), 'A Defence against the Public? Aspects of Intake in a Social Services Department', British Journal of Social Work, vol.12, no.6.
Akhurst, C. et al., (1980), 'Dear Priscilla Young ...', Community Care, no.318.
Alford, R., (1975), Health Care Politics, University of Chicago Press, Chicago.
Algie, J., (1970), 'Management and Organisation in the Social Services', British Hospital Journal and Social Services Review, vol.80.
Allen, V.L., (1975), Social Analysis: A Marxist Critique and Alternative, Longman, London.
Anthony, P.D., (1977), The Ideology of Work, Tavistock, London
Bailey, J., (1980), Ideas and Intervention: Social Theory for Practice, Routledge and Kegan Paul, London.
Bamford, Terry, (1982), Managing Social Work, Tavistock, London.
Barclay Report, (1982), Social Workers, Their Role and Tasks, Bedford Square Press, London.
Barter, J., (1969), 'Management in Social Services', British Hospital Journal and Social Services Review, vol.79.
Bebbington, Andrew and Davies, Bleddyn, (1979), 'Social Workers and Client Numbers (Research Note)', British Journal of Social Work, vol.9, no.1.
Birch Report, (1976), Manpower and Training in the Social

Services (DHSS), HMSO, London.

Black, Jim, Bowl, Ric, Burns, Douglas, Critcher, Chas., Grant, Gordon and Stockford, Dick, (1983), *Social Work in Context: A Comparative Study of Three Social Services Teams*, Tavistock, London.

Blau, Peter and Schoenherr, Richard, (1971), *The Structure of Organisations*, Basic Books, New York.

Boardman, S.G., (1977), *Survey of Active Caseloads*, Clearing House for LA Social Services Research, Birmingham.

Booth, Tim, Martin, David and Melotte, Chris, (1980), *Specialisation: Issues in the Organisation of Social Work*, BASW Publications, Birmingham.

Bowey, Angela M., (1976), *The Sociology of Organisations*, Hodder and Stoughton, London.

Braverman, Harry, (1974), *Labour and Monopoly Capital: The Degradation of Work in the Twentieth Century*, Monthly Review Press, New York.

Brearley, C. Paul, (1975), *Social Work, Ageing and Society*, Routledge and Kegan Paul, London.

Brewer, C. and Lait, J., (1980), *Can Social Work Survive?* Temple Smith, London.

Brogden, Mike and Wright, Mike, (1979), 'Reflection on the Social Work Strikes', *New Society*, 4 October, pp.14-16.

Burns, T. and Stalker, G.M., (1961), *The Management of Innovation*, Tavistock, London.

Burrell, Gibson and Morgan, Gareth, (1979), *Sociological Paradigms and Organisational Analysis*, Heinemann, London.

Butrym, Z.T., (1976), *The Nature of Social Work*, Macmillan, London.

Cain, Maureen, (1979), 'The General Practice Lawyer and the Client: towards a radical conception', in Dingwall, R. and Lewis, P., (eds), (1983).

Carchedi, G., (1977), *On the Economic Identification of Social Classes*, Routledge and Kegan Paul, London.

Carpenter, Michael, (1977), 'The New Managerialism and Professionalism in Nursing', in Stacey, Margaret et al., (eds), (1977), *Health and the Division of Labour*, Croom Helm, London.

Carpenter, Mick, (1978), 'Managerialism and the Division of Labour in Nursing', in Dingwall, Robert and McIntosh, Jean, (eds), (1978), *Readings in the Sociology of Nursing*, Churchill Livingstone, Edinburgh.

Carver, V. and Edwards, J., (1972), *Social Workers and their Workloads*, NISW, London.

Cawson, Alan, (1982), *Corporatism and Welfare: Social Policy and State Intervention in Britain*, Heinemann, London.

CCETSW, (1983), *Review of Qualifying Training Policies: Report of Council Working Group (Paper 20:1)*, CCETSW, London.

Challis, D. and Davies, B., (1980), 'A New Approach to Community Care for the Elderly', *British Journal of Social Work*, vol.10, no.1.

Child, J., (1972), 'Organisation, Structure and Strategies of Control', <u>Administrative Science Quarterly</u>, vol.17.
Clark, Burton R., (1956), 'Organizational Adaptation and Precarious Values: a case study', <u>American Sociological Review</u>, pp.327-36.
Clegg, Stewart, (1979), <u>The Theory of Power and Organisation</u>, Routledge and Kegan Paul, London.
Cohen, S., (1975), 'It's all right for you to talk', in Bailey, R. and Brake, M., (eds), (1975), <u>Radical Social Work</u>, Edward Arnold, London.
Conway, Freda, (1967), <u>Sampling: An Introduction for Social Scientists</u>, George Allen and Unwin, London.
Corby, Brian, (1982), 'Theory and Practice in Long Term Social Work: a case study of practice with SSD clients', <u>British Journal of Social Work</u>, vol.12, no.6.
Corrigan, P. and Leonard, P., (1978), <u>Social Work Practice under Capitalism</u>, Macmillan, London.
Crompton, R. and Jones, G., (1984), <u>White-Collar Proletariat</u>, Macmillan, London.
Crosbie, David, (1983), 'A Role for Anyone? A description of social work with the elderly; in two Area Offices', <u>British Journal of Social Work</u>, vol.13, no.2.
Crousaz, Dione, (1981), <u>Social Work: A Research Review</u>, HMSO, London.
Crozier, Michel, (1964), <u>The Bureaucratic Phenomenon</u>, Tavistock, London.
Davies, Martin, (1981), <u>The Essential Social Worker</u>, Heinemann, London.
DHSS, (1975), 'The Service Delivery Study', <u>Social Work Service</u>, June, no.6, pp.1-22.
Dingwall, Robert, Eekalaar, John and Murray, Topsy, (1983), <u>The Protection of Children</u>, Blackwell, Oxford.
Downie, R.S. and Loudfoot, E.M., (1978), 'Aim, Skill and Role in Social Work', in Timms, N. and Watson, D., (eds), (1978), <u>Philosophy in Social Work</u>, Routledge and Kegan Paul, London.
Duncan, R.B., (1972), 'Characteristics of Organizational Environments in Perceived Environmental Uncertainty', <u>Administrative Science Quarterly</u>, vol.17.
Dunsire, Andrew, (1978), <u>Control in a Bureaucracy</u>, Martin Robertson, Oxford.
Easthope, Gary, (1975), <u>Community, Hierarchy and Open Education</u>, Routledge and Kegan Paul, London.
Edwards, R.C., Gordon, D.M. and Reich, M., (eds), (1975), <u>Labour Market Segmentation</u>, D.C. Heath, Lexington.
Esland, Geoff, (1976), <u>Diagnoses and Therapy</u>, Unit 12, Block 4, Part 1, 'Politics of Work and Occupation', DE 351, Open University Press, Milton Keynes.
Etzioni, A., (ed.), (1969), <u>The Semi-Professions and their Organisation</u>, Free Press, New York.
Farmer, M., Holgate, E., Keidan, O. and Flynn, A., (1977), 'The

Independent Social Work Agency. A Report on the First Year of an Experiment in Social Casework', British Journal of Social Work, vol.7, no.3.

Finch, Wilbur A., (1976), 'Social Workers versus Bureaucracy' Social Work, Sept.

Fischer, Joel, (1973), 'Is Casework Effective? A Review', Social Work, vol.18, no.1

Flexner, A., (1915), 'Is Social Work a Profession?', Proceedings of the National Conference of Charities and Corrections, Hildman, New York.

Fox, Alan, (1974), Beyond Contract, Faber and Faber, London.

Freidson, E., (1970), Professional Dominance, Atherton, New York.

Friedman, L. Andrew, (1977), Industry and Labour, Macmillan, London.

Giddens, Anthony and Mackenzie, Gavin, (eds), (1982), Social Class and the Division of Labour, Cambridge University Press, Cambridge

Glastonbury, Bryan, Cooper, David and Hawkins, Pearl, (eds), (1980), Social Work in Conflict, Croom Helm, London.

Goldberg, E.M. and Connelly, N., (eds), (1981), Evaluative Research in Social Care, Heinemann, London.

Goldberg, E.M. and Fruin, D.J., (1976), 'Towards Accountability in Social Work: a case review system for social workers', British Journal of Social Work, vol.6, no.1.

Goldberg, E.M. and Hatch, Stephen, (eds), (1981), A New Look at the Personal Social Services, Discussion Paper no.4, PSI, London.

Goldberg, E.M., Mortimer, A. and Williams, B., (1970), Helping the Aged: A Field Experiment in Social Work, George Allen and Unwin, London.

Goldberg, E. Matilda and Warburton, R. William, (1979), Ends and Means in Social Work, George Allen and Unwin, London.

Goldberg, E.M., Warburton, R.W., Lyons, L.J. and Willmott, R.R., (1978), 'Towards Accountability in Social Work: long term social work in an Area Office', British Journal of Social Work, vol.8, no.3.

Goldberg, E.M., Warburton, R.W., McGuiness, B. and Rowlands, J.H., (1977), 'Towards Accountability in Social Work: one year's intake to an Area Office', British Journal of Social Work, vol.7, no.3.

Goldstein, Howard, (1973), Social Work Practice: A Unitary Approach, University of South Carolia Press, Columbia.

Goldthorpe, John, (1982), 'On the Service Class, its Formation and Future', in Giddens, A. and Mackenzie, G., (eds), (1982).

Gough, I., (1979), Political Economy of the Welfare State, Macmillan, London.

Gould, A., (1980), 'The Salaried Middle Class in the Corporatist Welfare State', Policy and Politics, vol.9.

Gouldner, A.W., (1971), The Coming Crisis of Western Sociology,

Heinemann, London.
Gouldner, A.W., (1976), *The Dialectic of Ideology and Technology*, Macmillan, London.
Greengross, Sally, (1980), 'Progression and Change in Thought and Practice in Work with the Elderly', in Booth, Tim, Martin, David and Melotte, Chris, (1980).
Greenwood, E., (1957), 'Attributes of a Profession', *Social Work*, 2 July.
Hadley, R. and McGrath, M., (eds), (1981), *Going Local: Neighbourhood Social Services*, National Council for Voluntary Associations, London.
Hage, Jerald and Aiken, Michael, (1969), 'Routine Technology, Social Structure and Organisational Goals', *Administrative Science Quarterly*, no.14, Sept.
Hall, C.S. and Lindzey, G., (1957), *Theories of Personality*, Chapman and Hall, London.
Ham, C.J., (1982), *Health Policy in Britain*, Macmillan, London.
Ham, Christopher and Hill, Michael, (1984), *The Policy Process in the Modern Capitalist State*, Wheatsheaf, Brighton.
Hardiker, Pauline, (1981), 'Heart or Head: the function and role of knowledge in social work', *Issues in Social Work Education*, vol.1, no.2.
Harris, John, (1979) 'More than Going Grey: a preliminary examination of gerontological theory and social work practice with old people', MA Thesis (Sociology), University of Warwick.
Hazel, Nancy, (1981), *A Bridge to Independence*, Blackwell, Oxford.
Hazel, Nancy, (1982), 'Regulating Family Placement', *Adoption and Fostering*, vol.6, no.3.
Hesse, Mary, (1978), 'Theory and Value in the Social Sciences' in Hookaway, C. and Pettit, P., (eds), (1978), *Action and Interpretation*, Cambridge University Press, Cambridge.
Hey, Anthea, (1979), 'Specialisation in Social Work' in Cypher, John, (ed.), (1979), *Seebohm: Across Three Decades*, BASW Publications, Birmingham.
Hey, Anthea, (1982) 'Third Time Lucky', *Community Care*, 14 January.
Hill, Stephen, (1981), *Competition and Control at Work*, Heinemann, London.
Holman, R., (1976), *Inequality in Child Care*, Poverty Pamphlet no.26, CPAG, London.
Holme, A. and Maizels, J., (1978), *Social Workers and Volunteers*, George Allen and Unwin, London.
Hope, Mary, (1977), Letter to *Social Work Today*, 25 January, p.26.
Howe, David, (1979), 'Agency Function and Social Work Principles', *British Journal of Social Work*, vol.9, no.1.
Howe, David, (1983), 'The Social Work Imagination in Practice and Education', *Issues in Social Work Education*, vol.3, no.2.

Hughes, Everett C., (1958), *Men and Their Work*, Free Press, New York.
Hughes, Everett C., (1971), *The Sociological Eye: Selected Papers*, Aldine-Atherton, Chicago.
Illich, Ivan, (1977), *Limits to Medicine*, Penguin, London
Illich, Ivan et al., (1977), *Disabling Professionals*, Marion Boyers, London
Jeans, M.S., (1978), *Role Analysis in Field Social Work: The Development of a New Model*, Devon County Council Social Services Department, Exeter.
Johnson, Terence J., (1972), *Professions and Power*, Macmillan, London.
Johnson, Terence J., (1973), 'The Professions', in Hurd, Geoffrey, (ed.), (1973), *Human Societies*, Routledge and Kegan Paul, London.
Johnson, Terence, (1977), 'The Professions in the Class Structure', in Scase, Richard, (ed.), (1977), *Industrial Society: Class Cleavage and Control*, George Allen and Unwin, London.
Johnson, Terry, (1982), 'The State and the Professions: Peculiarities of the British', in Giddens, A. and Mackenzie, G., (eds), (1982).
Jones, Chris, (1983), *State Social Work and the Working Class*, Macmillan, London.
Julia, Angela, (1978), 'The Professional Development of the Social Worker's Role with the Mentally Disordered', *Social Work Service*, May.
Kakabadse, A., (1982), *Culture of the Social Services*, Gower, Aldershot.
Katz, Fred E., (1969), 'Nurses', in Etzioni, A.
Larson, Margali S., (1977), *The Rise of the Professions*, University of California Press, Berkeley.
Lee, Phil, (1982), 'Some Contemporary and Perennial Problems of Relating Theory to Practice in Social Work', in Bailey, Roy and Lee, Phil, (eds), (1982), *Theory and Practice in Social Work*, Blackwell, Oxford.
Leonard, Peter, (1973), 'Professionalisation, Community Action and the Growth of Social Service Bureaucracies'. in Halmos, Paul, (ed.), (1973), *Professionalism and Social Change*, Sociological Review Monograph no.20, University of Keele, Keele.
Leonard, Peter, (1978), 'Which Way for the Personal Social Services?', *Social Work Service*, no.18.
Lipsky, M., (1980), *Street-Level Bureaucracy*, Russell Sage, New York.
Littler, Craig R., (1982), *The Development of the Labour Process in Capitalist Societies*, Heinemann, London.
Lukes, Steven, (1974), *Power: A Radical View*, Macmillan, London.
McAuley, Patricia, Catherwood, Mary-Louis, Bolton, Rosemary and Campbell, Desmond, (1983), 'The Social Work Task in an Acute

Psychiatric In-Patient Unit', British Journal of Social Work, vol.13, no.6.
McCleary, R., (1975), 'How Structural Variables Constrain the Parole Officer's Use of Discretionary Powers', Social Problems, vol.23, no.2.
McCreadie, Claudine, (1977), 'The Social Services', in Jones, Kathleen, (ed.), (1977), The Year Book of Social Policy, Routledge and Kegan Paul, London.
McKinlay, John B., (1975), Processing People: Cases in Organisational Behaviour, Holt, Rinehart, London.
McKnight, John, (1977), 'Professionalised Service and Disabling Help', in Illich, I., (1977).
Mant, Alistair, (1979), The Rise and Fall of the British Manager, Pan Books, London.
Mattinson, Janet and Sinclair, Ian, (1979), Mate and Stalemate: Working with Marital Problems in a Social Services Department, Blackwell, Oxford.
Miller, H., (1968), 'Value Dilemmas in Social Casework', Social Work, Jan.
Mishra, Ramesh, (1981), Society and Social Policy (2nd edition), Macmillan, London.
Mullen, E.J. and Dumpson, J.R., (1973), Evaluation of Social Intervention, Jossey-Bass, San Francisco.
Neill, June, (1982), 'Some Variations in Policy and Procedure relating to Part 3 Applications in the GLC Area', British Journal of Social Work, vol.12, no.3.
Neill, June E. et al., (1973), 'Reactions to Integration: the views and attitudes of social workers in a newly reorganised Social Services Department', Social Work Today, vol.4, no.14, 1 November, pp.458-65.
Neill, June E., Warburton, R.W. and McGuiness, Brendan, (1976), 'Post-Seebohm Services: (1) The Social Worker's Viewpoint', Social Work Today, 2 November, vol.8, no.5.
Nokes, Peter, (1967), The Professional Task in Welfare Practice, Routledge and Kegan Paul, London.
O'Connor, James, (1973), The Fiscal Crisis of the State, St. Martin's Press, New York.
Offe, Claus, (1976), Industry and Inequality, Edward Arnold, London.
Parry, Noel and Parry, Jose, (1979), 'Social Work, Professionalism and the State', in Parry, Noel, Rustin, Michael and Satyamurti, Carole, (eds), (1979).
Parry, Noel, Rustin, Michael and Satyamurti, Carole, (eds), (1979), Social Work, Welfare and the State, Edward Arnold, London.
Parton, Nigel, (1979), 'The Natural History of Child Abuse: a study in social problem definition', British Journal of Social Work, vol.9, no.4.
Parton, Nigel, (1981), 'Child Abuse, Social Anxiety and Welfare', British Journal of Social Work, vol.11, no.4.

Payne, Malcolm, (1979), Power, Authority and Responsibility in Social Services: Social Work in Area Teams, Macmillan, London.
Pearson, G., (1973), 'Social Work as the Privatised Solution to Public Ills', British Journal of Social Work, vol.3, no.2.
Pearson, G., (1975), 'The Politics of Uncertainty', in Jones, H. (ed.), Towards a New Social Work, Routledge and Kegan Paul, London.
Perrow, Charles, (1965), 'Hospitals: Technology, Structure and Goals', in Perrow, Charles, (ed.), (1965), Handbook of Organisations, Rand McNally, Chicago.
Perrow, C., (1972), The Radical Attack on Business, Harcourt Brace Javanovich, New York.
Peters, R.S., (1966), Ethics and Education, George Allen and Unwin, London,
Pfeffer, Jeffrey, (1981), Power in Organisations, Pitman, Marshfield, Mass.
Philp, Mark, (1979), 'Notes on the Form of Knowledge in Social Work', Sociological Review, vol.27, no.1.
Piliavin, I., (1968), 'Restructuring the Provision of Social Services', Social Work, Jan.
Pinker, Robert, (1971), Social Theory and Social Policy, Heinemann, London.
Pinker, Robert, (1982), 'An Alternative View: Appendix B', in Barclay Report, (1982).
Pinker, Robert, (1984), 'Populism and the Social Services', Social Policy and Administration, vol.18, no.1.
Prottas, J.M., (1979), People Processing, Lexington Books, Lexington, Mass.
Pugh, D.S. and Hickson, D.J., (1976), Organisational Structure in its Context, Saxon House, Farnborough.
Rees, Stuart, (1978), Social Work Face to Face, Edward Arnold, London.
Reid, W. and Hanrahan, P., (1981), 'The Effectiveness of Social Work: Recent Evidence', in Goldberg, E.M. and Connelly, N., (eds), (1981).
Renner, K., (1953), 'Wandlungen der modernen Gesellschaft, Vienna', quoted in Giddens, A. and Mackenzie, G., (eds), (1982).
Rowlings, Cherry, (1981), Social Work with Elderly People, George Allen and Unwin, London.
Rueschmeyer, Dietrich, (1964), 'Doctors and Lawyers: A Comment on the Theory of Professions', The Canadian Review of Sociology and Anthropology, 1 February.
Rueschmeyer, Dietrich, (1973), Lawyers and their Society: A Comparative Study of the Legal Profession in Germany and in the United States, Harvard University Press, Cambridge, Mass.
Rueschmeyer, Dietrich, (1983), 'Professional Autonomy and the Social Control of Expertise', in Dingwall, R. and Lewis, P., (eds), (1983).
Salaman, Graeme, (1978), 'Towards a Sociology of Organizational

Structure', *The Sociological Review*, vol.26, no.3.
Salaman, Graeme, (1979), *Work Organisations: Resistance and Control*, Longman, London.
Salaman, Graeme, (1980), 'Classification of Organisations and Organisation Structure', in Salaman, G. and Thompson, K., (eds), (1980).
Salaman, Graeme, (1981), *Class and the Corporation*, Fontana, Glasgow.
Salaman, Graeme, (1982), 'Managing the Frontier of Control', in Giddens, A. and Mackenzie, G., (eds), (1982).
Salaman, Graeme and Thompson, Kenneth, (eds), (1980), *Control and Ideology in Organisations*, The Open University Press, Milton Keynes.
Satyamurti, Carole, (1981), *Occupational Survival*, Blackwell, Oxford.
Scott, Robert A., (1970), 'The Construction of Concepts of Stigma by Professional Experts', in Douglas, J.D., (ed.), (1970), *Deviance and Respectability: The Social Construction of Moral Meanings*, Basic Books, New York.
Seebohm Report, (1968), *Report of the Committee on Local Authority and Allied Personal Social Services*, Cmnd 3703, HMSO, London.
Shaw, Ian and Walton, R., (1978), 'What Use Social Work Training?', *Community Care*, 18 January.
Sheldon, Brian, (1978), 'Theory and Practice in Social Work: a re-examination of a tenuous relationship', *British Journal of Social Work*, vol.8, no.1.
Shortell, Stephen M., (1977), 'The Role of Environment in a Configurational Theory of Organisations', *Human Relations*, vol.30, no.3.
Simpkin, M., (1979), *Trapped within Welfare*, Macmillan, London.
Smith, Gilbert, (1981), 'Discretionary-Decision Making in Social Work', in Adler, Michael and Asquith, Stewart, (1981), *Discretion and Welfare*, Heinemann, London.
Smith, Gilbert and Ames, Janet, (1976), 'Area Teams in Social Work Practice: a programme for research', *British Journal of Social Work*, vol.6, no.1.
Standing Conference Certificate in Social Service, (1983), 'A Model for an Integrated System of Education and Training for the Personal Social Services', London, December.
Stevenson, Olive, (1978), 'Seebohm - 7 years on', *New Society*, 2 February.
Stevenson, Olive, (1981), *Specialisation in Social Service Teams*, George Allen and Unwin, London.
Stevenson, Olive and Parsloe, Phyllida, (1978), *Social Service Teams: The Practitioners' View*, DHSS, London
Thorpe, D., (1977), 'Analysis and Evaluation of IT Programmes', NITF Conference Papers.
Thorpe, D., (1979), 'IT: a service for the kids or the courts?', *Rapport*, February.

Thorpe, D., Paley, J. and Green, C., (1979), 'The Making of a Delinquent', Community Care, 26 April.

Thorpe, D., Smith, D., Green, C. and Paley, J., (1980), Out of Care: The Community Support of Juvenile Offenders, George Allen and Unwin, London.

Timms, Noel and Timms, Rita, (1977), Perspectives in Social Work, Routledge and Kegan Paul, London.

Titmuss, R.M., (1976), Commitment to Welfare, George Allen and Unwin, London.

Toren, Nina, (1972), Social Work: The Case of a Semi-Profession, Sage, London.

Vickery, Anne, (1973), 'Specialist: Generic: What next?', Social Work Today, vol.4, no.9, 26 July, pp.262-68.

Walsh, K., Hinings, R., Greenwood, R. and Ranson, S., (1981), 'Power and Advantage in Organisations', Organisation Studies, vol.2, no.2.

Walton, Ronald G., (1975), Women in Social Work, Routledge and Kegan Paul, London.

Ward, R., Fogg, R. and Pottage, D., (1973), Client Contact Survey, West Riding County Council Social Services Department, December.

Warham, Joyce, (1977), An Open Case: The Organisational Context of Social Work, Routledge and Kegan Paul, London.

Webb, Adrian and Wiston, Gerald, (1982), Whither State Welfare? Policy and Implementation in the PSS 1979-80, Royal Institute of Public Administration, London.

Weeks, David R., (1980), 'Organisations and Decision-Making', in Salaman, G. and Thompson, K., (eds), (1980).

Whittington, Colin, (1977), 'Social Workers' Orientations: an action perspective', British Journal of Social Work, vol.7, no.1.

Whittington, Colin, (1983), 'Social Work in the Welfare Network: negotiating daily practice', British Journal of Social Work, vol.13, no.3.

Wilding, Paul, (1982), Professional Power and Social Welfare, Routledge and Kegan Paul, London.

Wilensky, H., (1962), 'The Dynamics of Professionalism: the case of the hospital administrator', Hospital Administration, vol.7, no.2.

Wilkes, Ruth, (1981), Social Work with Undervalued Groups, Tavistock, London.

Woodward, J., (1969), 'Management and Technology', in Burns, T., (ed.), (1969), Industrial Man, Penguin, Harmondsworth.

Younghusband, E., (1951), Social Work in Britain: A Supplementary Report on the Employment and Training of Social Workers, Constable, Edinburgh.

Younghusband, E., (1978), Social Work in Britain: 1950-1975 Vol I, George Allen and Unwin, London.

Younghusband Report, (1959), Report of the Working Party on Social Workers in the Local Authority Health and Welfare Services, HMSO, London.